FIRST 50 BLUES SONGS

YOU SHOULD PLAY ON THE PIANO

ISBN 978-1-5400-5078-6

Visit Hal Leonard Online at
www.halleonard.com

Contact us:
Hal Leonard
7777 West Bluemound Road
Milwaukee, WI 53213
Email: info@halleonard.com

In Europe, contact:
Hal Leonard Europe Limited
42 Wigmore Street
Marylebone, London, W1U 2RN
Email: info@halleonardeurope.com

In Australia, contact:
Hal Leonard Australia Pty. Ltd.
4 Lentara Court
Cheltenham, Victoria, 3192 Australia
Email: info@halleonard.com.au

CONTENTS

AIN'T NO SUNSHINE

Words and Music by
BILL WITHERS

Slow Rock - Blues feel

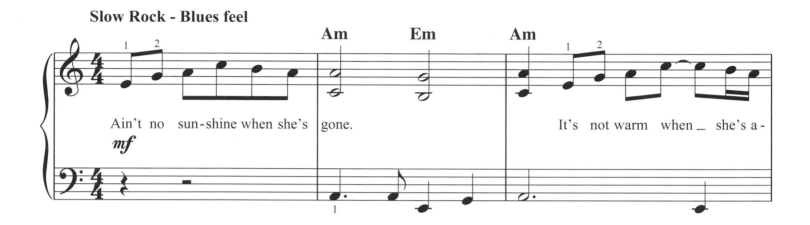

Ain't no sun-shine when she's gone.

mf

It's not warm when __ she's a-

way.

Ain't no sun-shine when she's gone, and she's al-ways gone too

long an-y-time __ she goes a-way.

Won-der this time where she's

gone,
gone,

won - der if she's __ gone to stay.)
on - ly dark - ness __ ev -'ry day.)

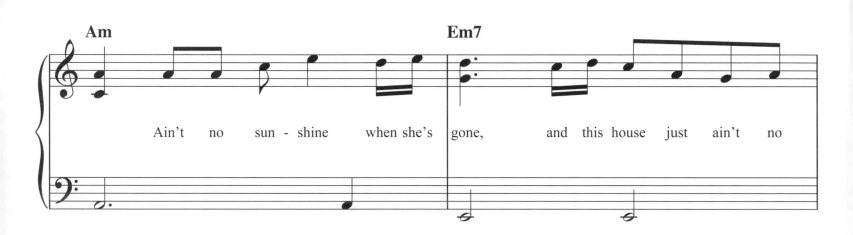

Ain't no sun - shine when she's gone, and this house just ain't no

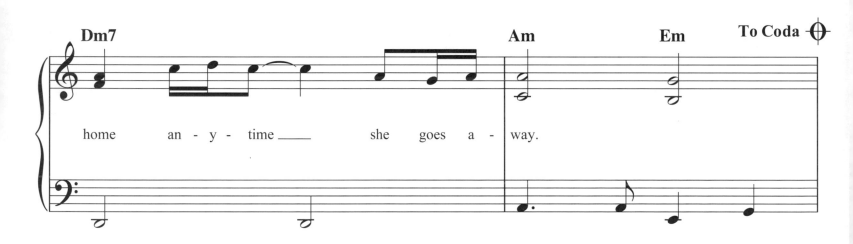

home an - y - time ____ she goes a - way.

To Coda ⊕

And I know, I know, I know, _ I know, I know, I know, I know, I know, I know, I

know, I know, __ I know, I know, I know, I know, __ I know, I know, I know, I know, I know,

Em

I know, I know, I know, I know, I know, I know, hey, I ought to leave the young thing a-

Am   **D.S. al Coda**

lone, but ain't no sun-shine when she's gone.   Ain't no sun-shine when she's

CODA

Am   **Em**   **Am**   **Am(add9)**

An-y- time __ she goes a- way.

ALL BLUES

By MILES DAVIS

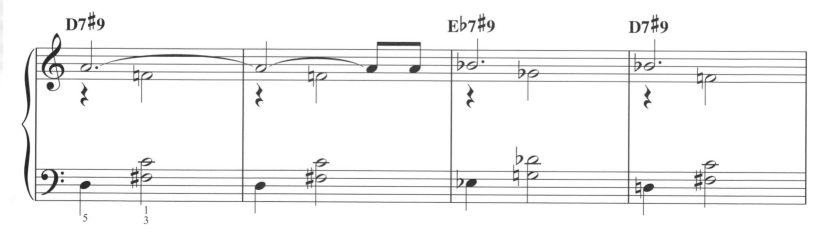

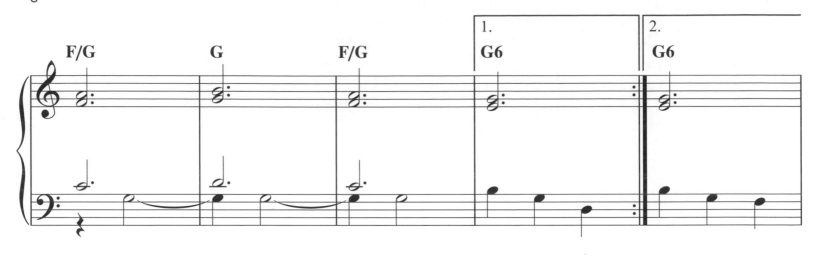

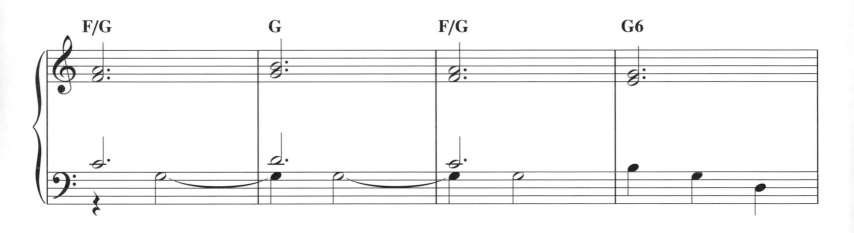

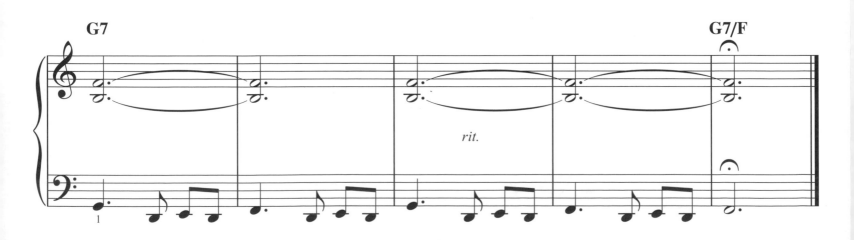

AT LAST
from ORCHESTRA WIVES

Lyric by MACK GORDON
Music by HARRY WARREN

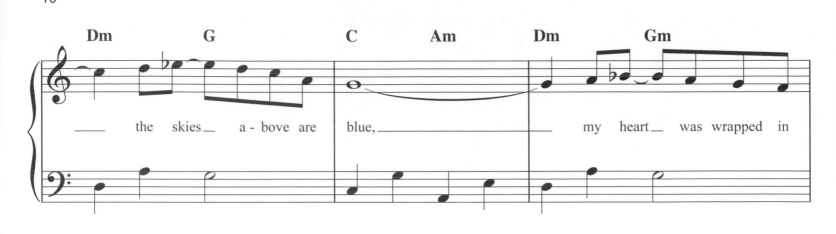

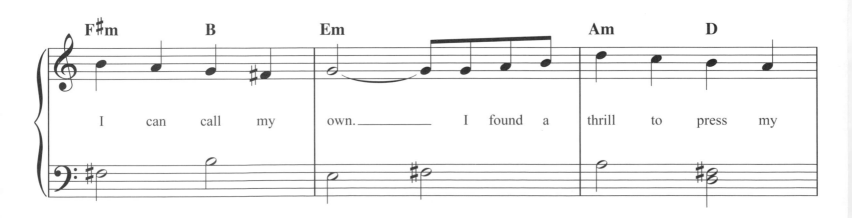

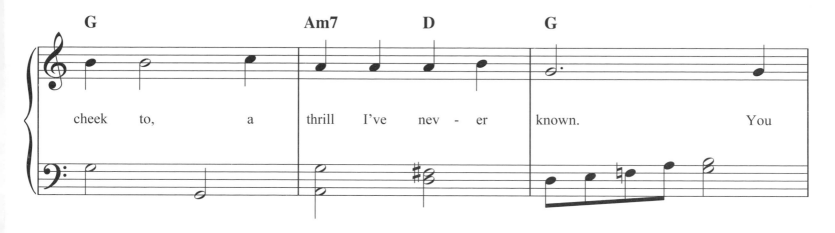

cheek to, a thrill I've nev - er known. You

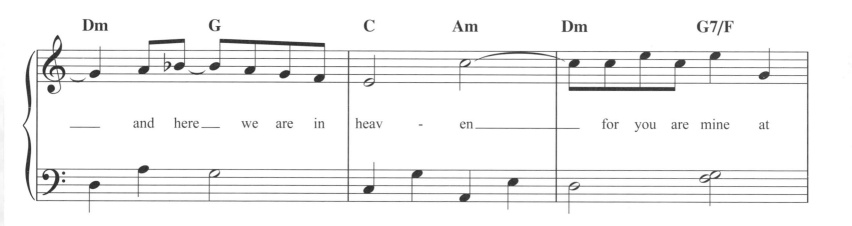

smiled _____ and then ___ the spell was cast _____

___ and here ___ we are in heav - en _____ for you are mine at

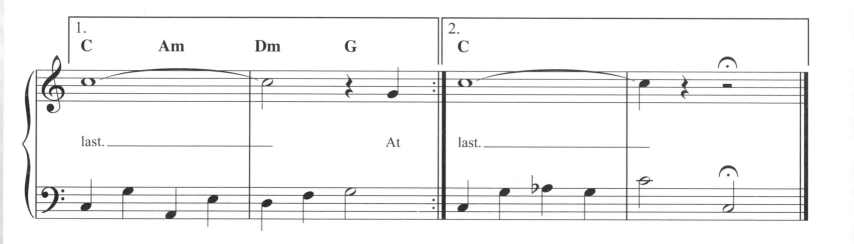

1.

last. _____ At

2.

last. _____

BLUEBERRY HILL

Words and Music by AL LEWIS,
LARRY STOCK AND VINCENT ROSE

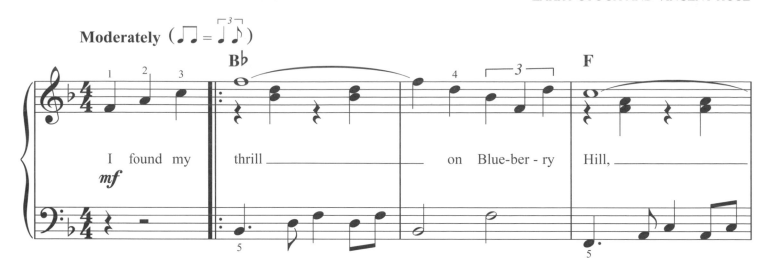

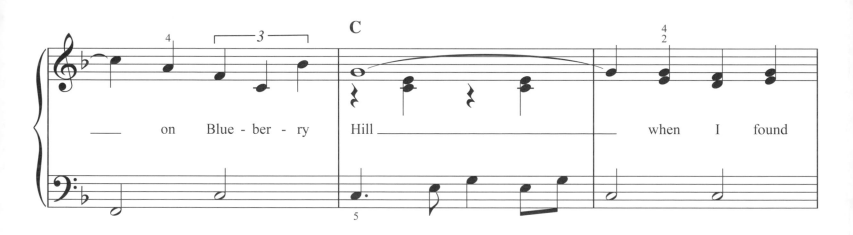

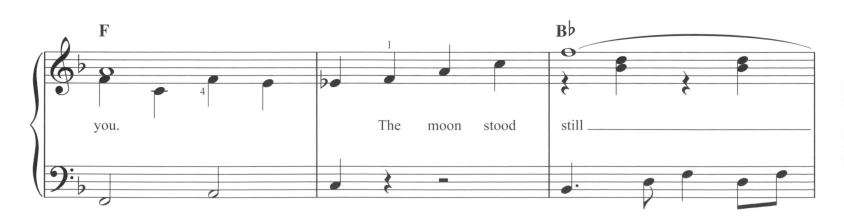

on Blue - ber - ry Hill _____ and lin - gered un -

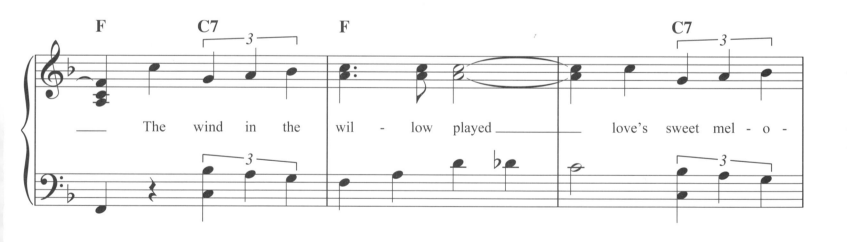

til _____ my dreams came true. _____

_____ The wind in the wil - low played _____ love's sweet mel - o -

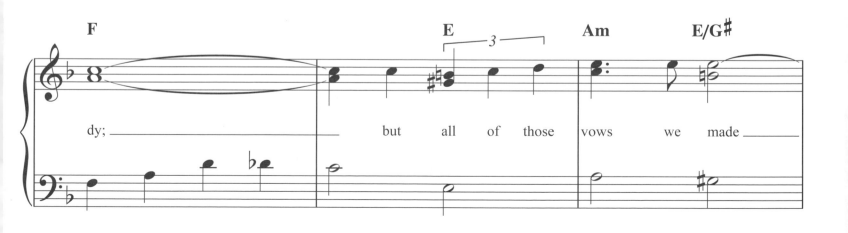

dy; _____ but all of those vows we made _____

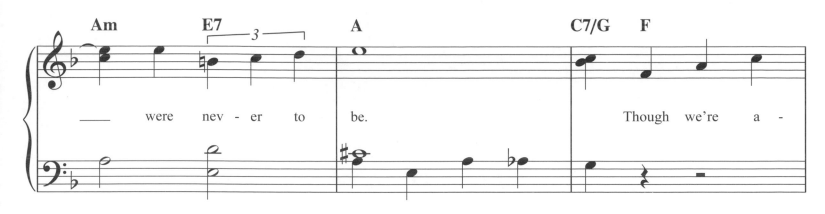

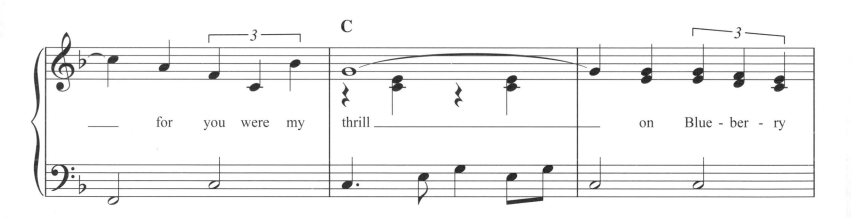

BABY PLEASE DON'T GO

Words and Music by
JOSEPH LEE WILLIAMS

16

BOOGIE WOOGIE STOMP

Words and Music by
ALBERT AMMONS

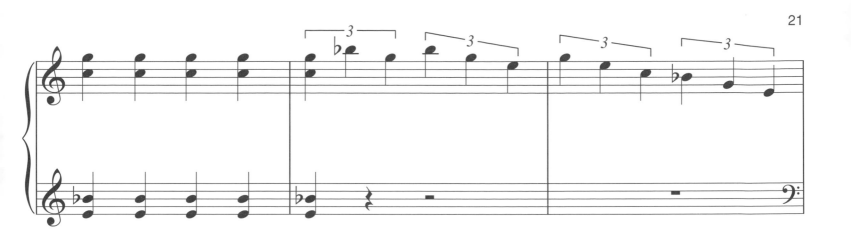

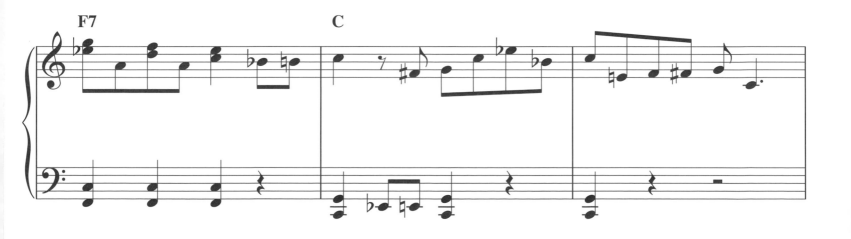

F7

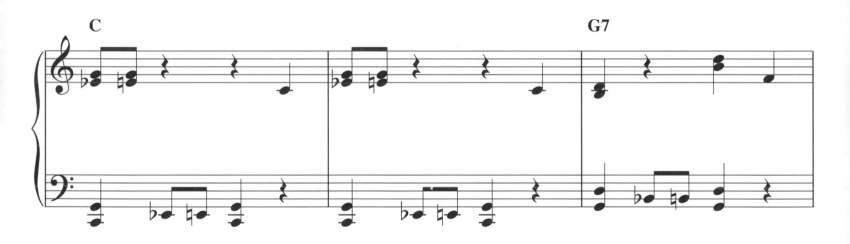

C   **G7**

F7   **C**

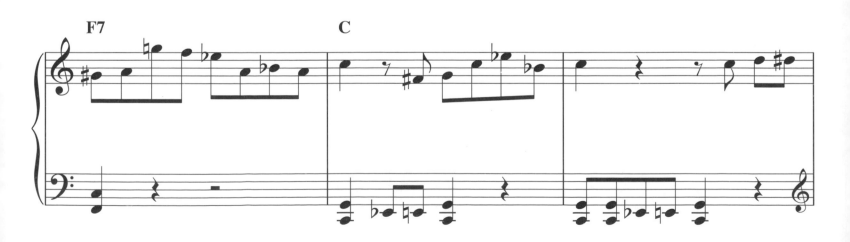

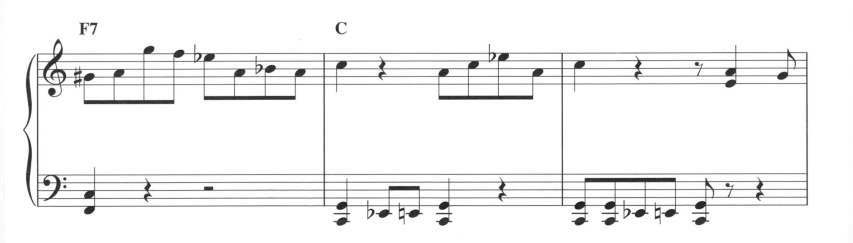

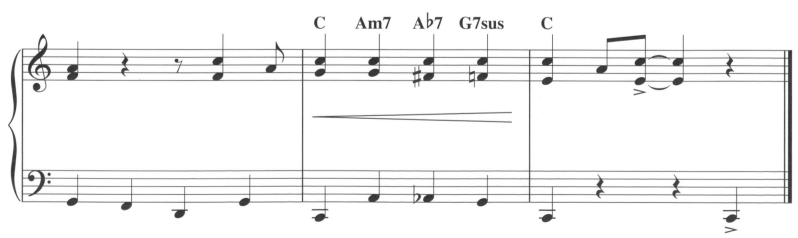

BASIN STREET BLUES

Words and Music by
SPENCER WILLIAMS

band's there to meet us,   old friends to greet us,

where all the light and the dark folks meet, __

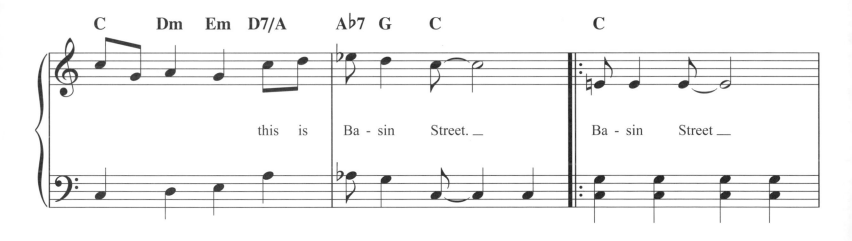

this is Ba - sin Street. __   Ba - sin Street __

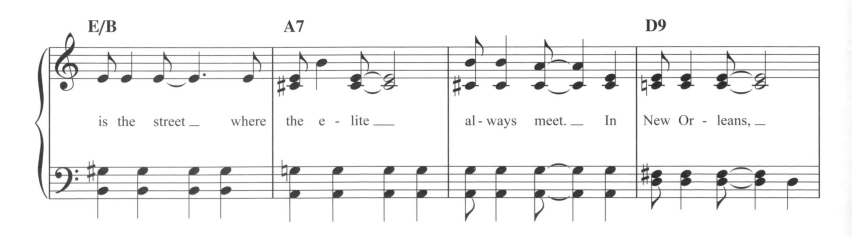

is the street __ where the e - lite __ al - ways meet. __ In New Or - leans, __

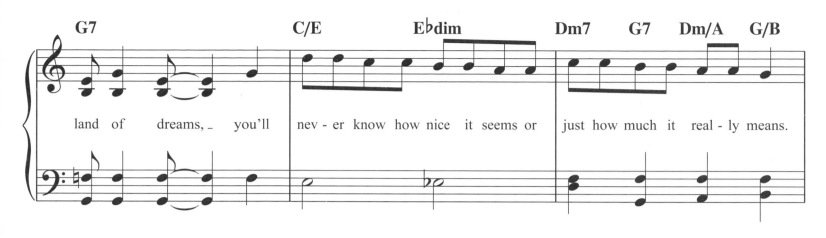

land of dreams, _ you'll nev - er know how nice it seems or just how much it real - ly means.

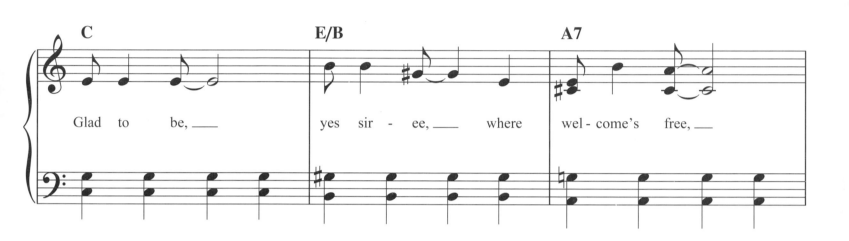

Glad to be, ____ yes sir - ee, ____ where wel - come's free, ___

dear to me, ___ where I can lose ___ my Ba - sin Street

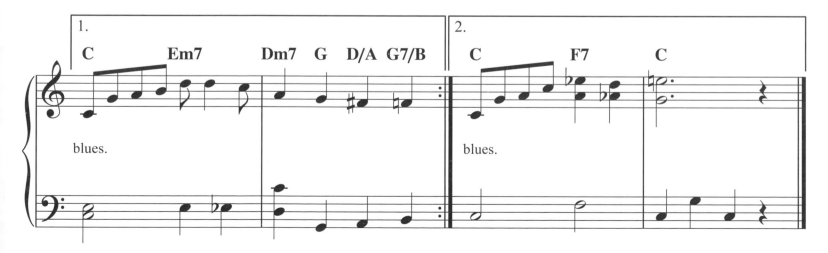

blues.   blues.

THE BIRTH OF THE BLUES
from GEORGE WHITE'S SCANDALS OF 1926

Words by B.G. DeSYLVA and LEW BROWN
Music by RAY HENDERSON

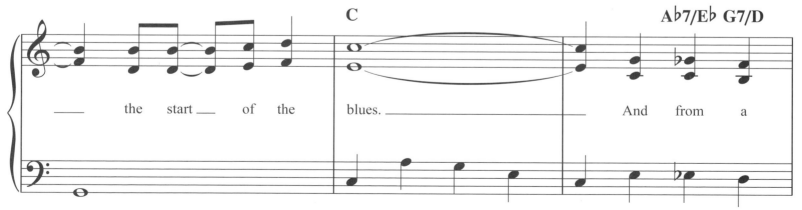

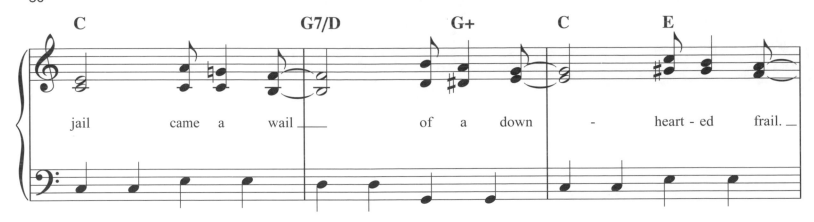

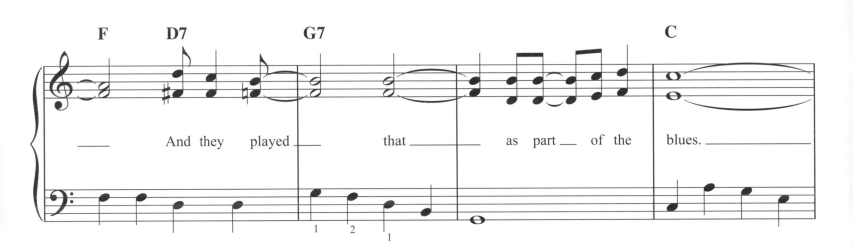

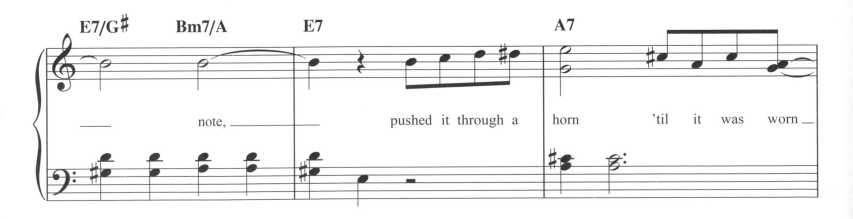

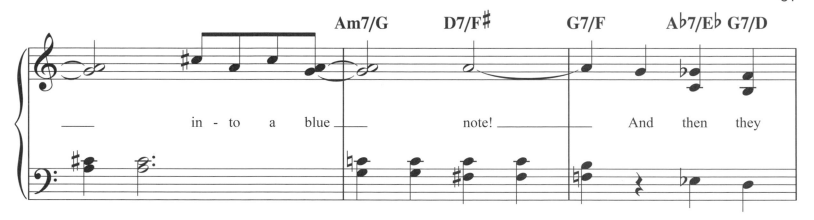

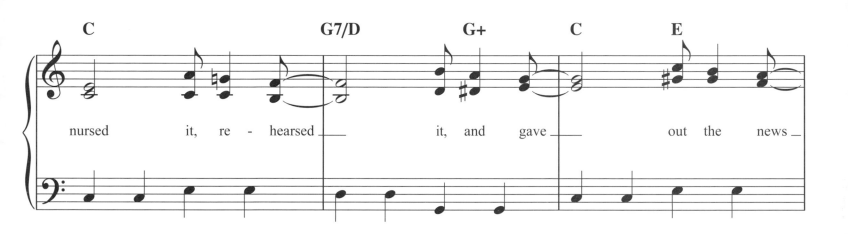

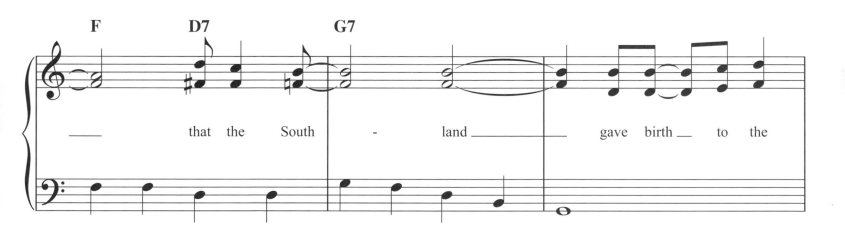

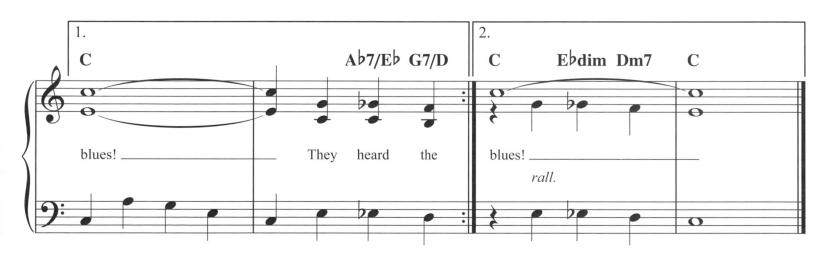

C-JAM BLUES

By DUKE ELLINGTON

Medium Swing

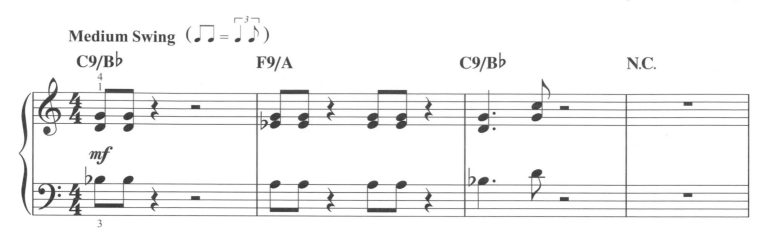

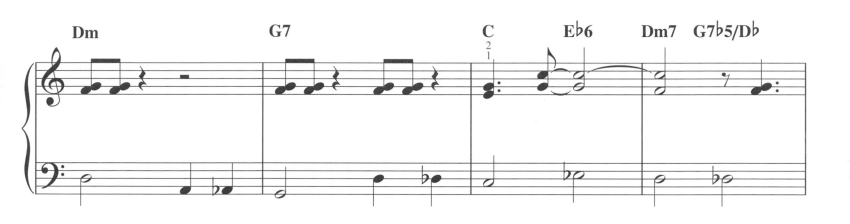

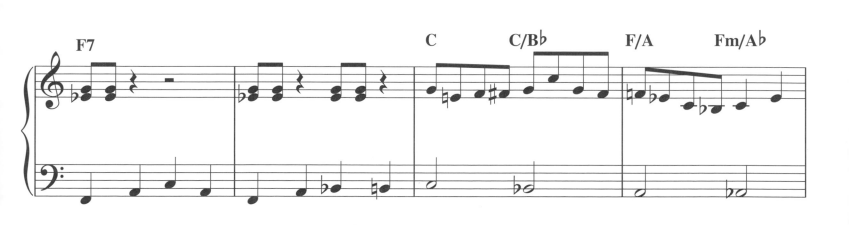

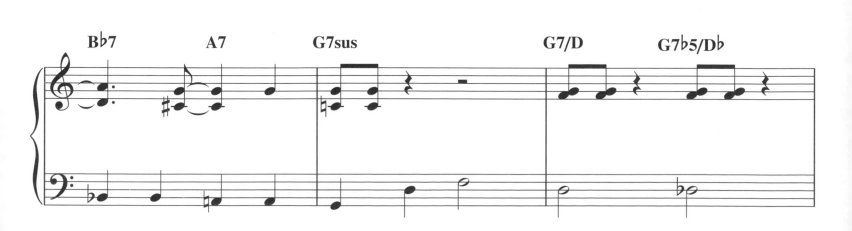

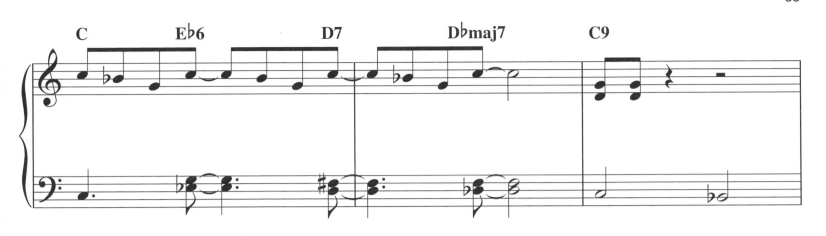

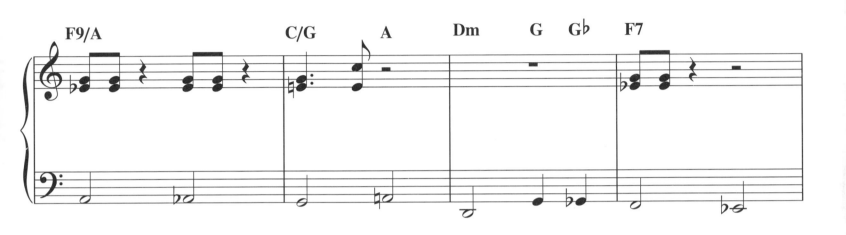

CALDONIA
(What Makes Your Big Head So Hard?)

Words and Music by
FLEECIE MOORE

Walk-in' with my ba-by, she's got great big feet;__ she's long, lean and lan-ky, ain't had

noth-in' to eat, but she's my ba-by, and I love her just the

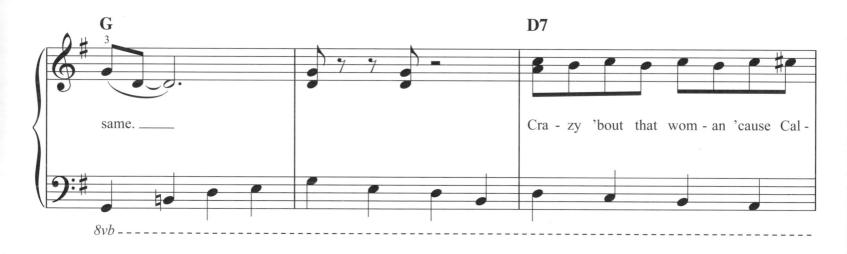

same.__ Cra-zy 'bout that wom-an 'cause Cal-

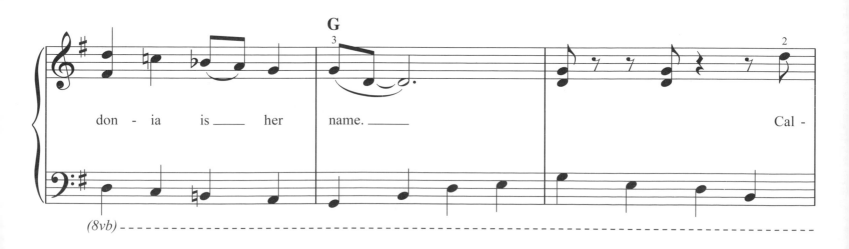

don-ia is__ her name.__ Cal-

G6

(Spoken:) My mama told me to | leave Caldonia alone; | "She's bad for your morale."

(8vb) -

C7

But mama didn't know | I loved Caldonia,

(8vb) -

G6　　　　　　　　　　　　　　　　**Am7**　　　　　　**D7**

she's such a swell gal! | So I'm goin' down to Caldonia's | house and ask her

8vb -

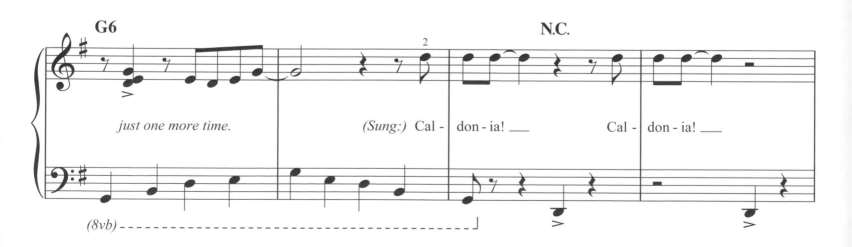

G6　　　　　　　　　　　　　　　　**N.C.**

just one more time. | *(Sung:)* Cal - don - ia! ___ | Cal - don - ia! ___

(8vb) -

What makes your big head so hard?

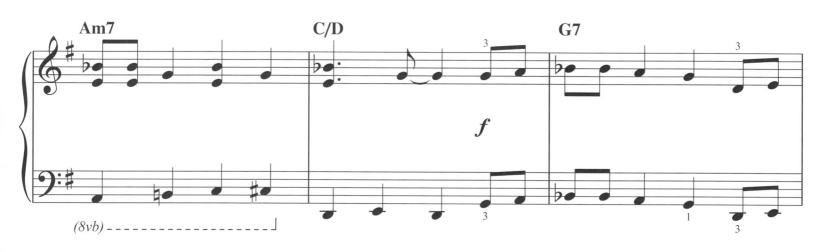

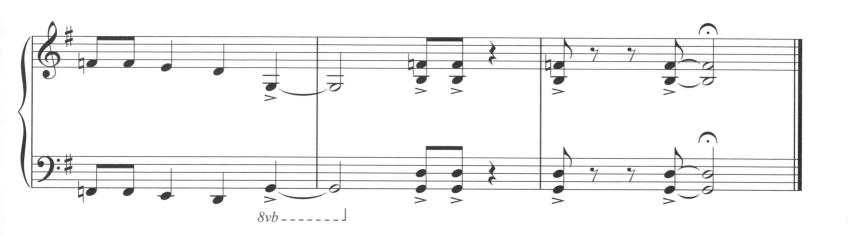

COW COW BLUES

Words and Music by
CHARLES DAVENPORT

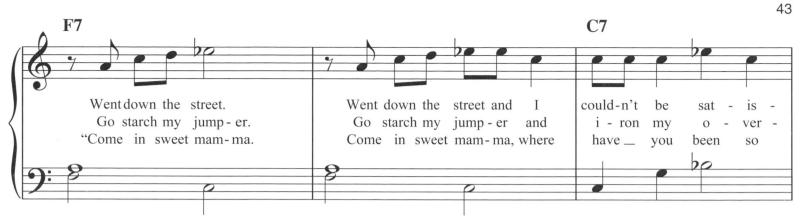

Went down the street.
Go starch my jump-er.
"Come in sweet mam-ma.

Went down the street and I
Go starch my jump-er and
Come in sweet mam-ma, where

could-n't be sat-is-
i-ron my o-ver-
have __ you been so

fied.
alls.
long?"

I had those rail-road blues
I'm goin' to ride that train
"I've been in Cin-cin-nat-i

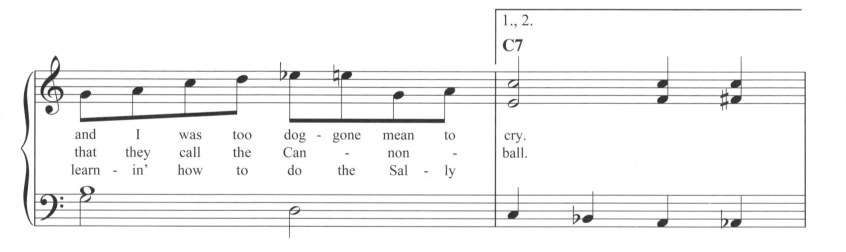

and I was too dog-gone mean to
that they call the Can-non-
learn-in' how to do the Sal-ly

cry.
ball.

1., 2.

Some
She

Long."

CROSS ROAD BLUES
(Crossroads)

Words and Music by
ROBERT JOHNSON

Bright Country Blues

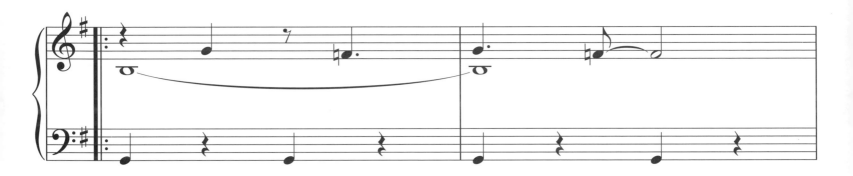

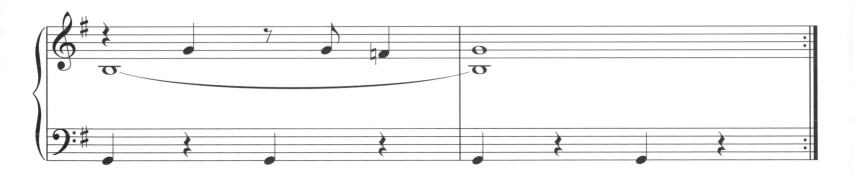

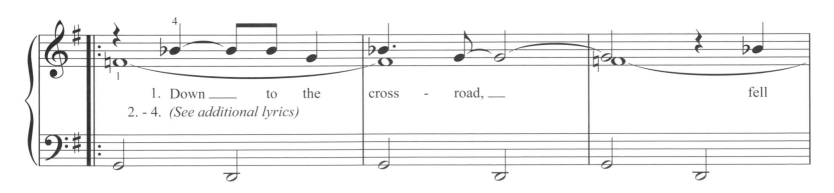

1. Down ___ to the cross - road, ___   fell
2. - 4. *(See additional lyrics)*

down on my knees. _____

C7

I went to the cross-

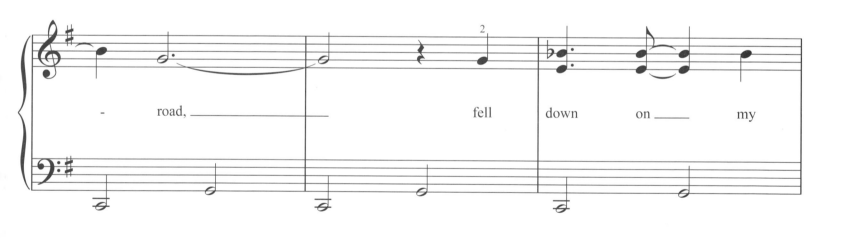

- road, _____ fell down on _____ my

G7

knees. _____

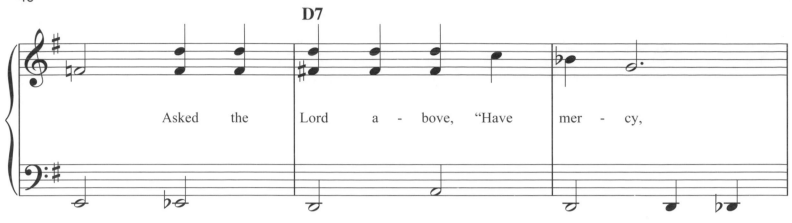

Asked the Lord a - bove, "Have mer - cy,

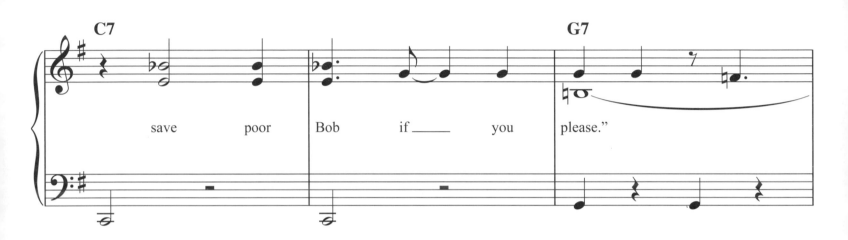

save poor Bob if _____ you please."

1., 2., 3.

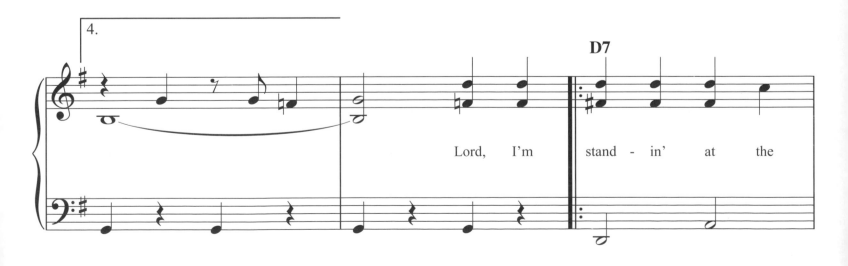

4.

Lord, I'm stand - in' at the

Additional Lyrics

2. Mmm, standin' at the crossroad, I tried to flag a ride.
   Standin' at the crossroad, I tried to flag a ride.
   Ain't nobody seem to know me, ev'rybody pass me by.

3. Mmm, the sun goin' down, boy, dark gon' catch me here.
   Ooh, the sun goin' down, boy, dark gon' catch me here.
   I haven't got no lovin' sweet woman that love and feel my care.

4. You can run, you can run, tell my friendboy Willie Brown.
   You can run, tell my friendboy Willie Brown, Lord,
   That I'm standin' at the crossroad, babe, I believe I'm sinkin' down.

DARLIN' YOU KNOW I LOVE YOU

Words and Music by B.B. KING
and JULES BIHARI

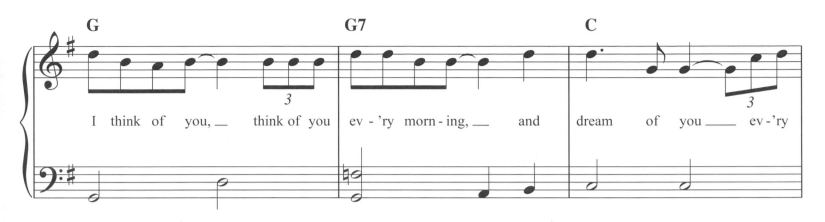

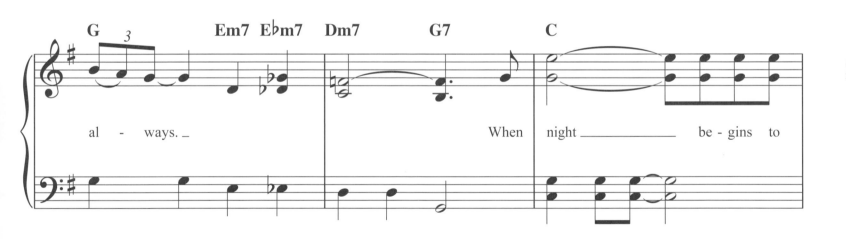

wish, ba-by, I could hold you _____ in my arms to-

night. Oh, _____ dar-lin', dar-lin', you know I love you. _____ I

love you _____ for my-self, but you've gone, gone _____ and

left me _____ for some-one else. _____ *mp*

EARLY IN THE MORNIN'

Words and Music by LEO HICKMAN,
LOUIS JORDAN and DALLAS BARTLEY

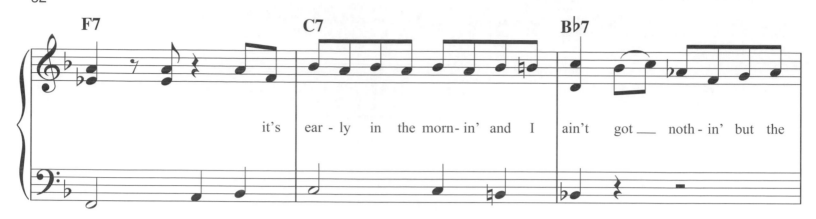

it's ear - ly in the morn- in' and I ain't got ___ noth- in' but the

blues. ___

I went to all the plac - es where we
I went to see her girl-friend but ___
had a lot of mon - ey when I

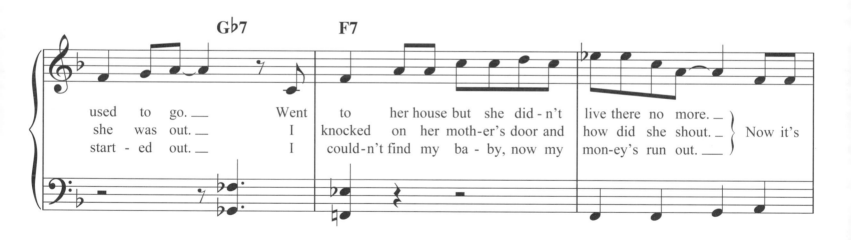

used to go. ___ Went to her house but she did - n't live there no more. ___
she was out. ___ I knocked on her moth-er's door and how did she shout. ___
start - ed out. ___ I could-n't find my ba - by, now my mon-ey's run out. ___

Now it's

ear - ly in the morn- in', it's ear - ly in the morn- in',

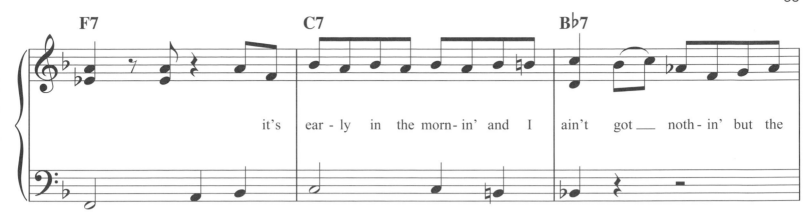

it's ear-ly in the morn-in' and I ain't got ___ noth-in' but the

blues. _____ I

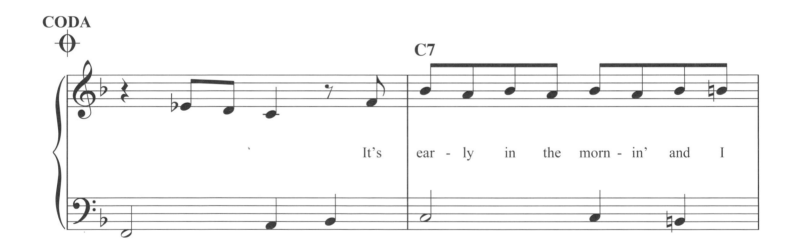

CODA

It's ear-ly in the morn-in' and I

ain't got ___ noth-in' but the blues. _____

EVERY DAY I HAVE THE BLUES

Words and Music by
PETER CHATMAN

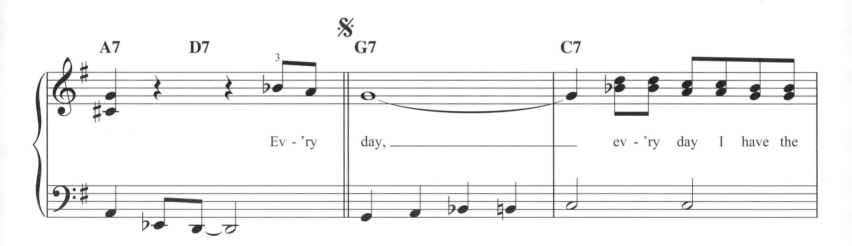

me, no-bod-y seems to ___ care;   speak-in' of

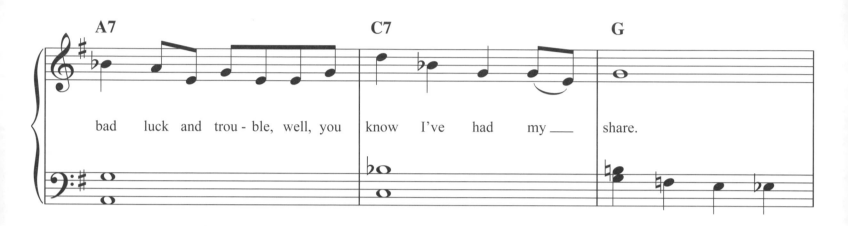

bad   luck and trou-ble, well, you   know I've had   my ___ share.

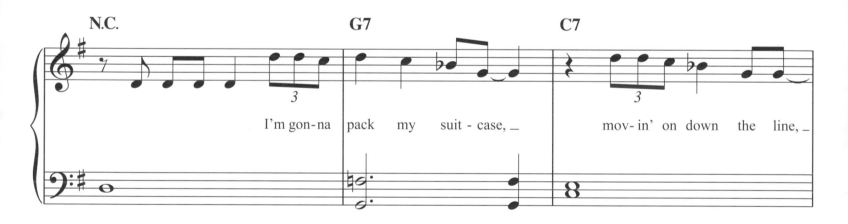

I'm gon-na pack   my   suit-case, ___   mov-in' on down   the   line, ___

___   I'm gon-na   pack   my   suit-case,

C#dim　　　　　　　**G**　　　　　　　**Bm7♭5**　　　**E**

move on down the ___ line,　　　　　　　well, there ain't

A7　　　　　　　**C7**　　　　　　　**G**

no - bod - y wor - ryin' and there ain't no - bod - y cryin'.

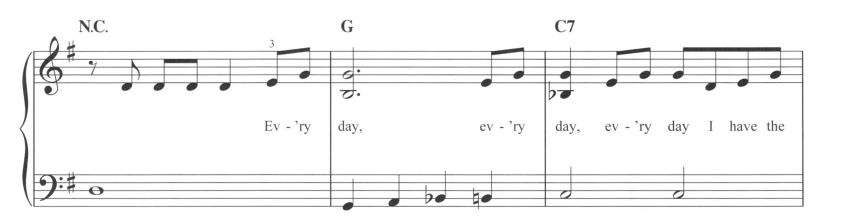

N.C.　　　　　　　**G**　　　　　**C7**

Ev - 'ry day,　　　　ev - 'ry day, ev - 'ry day I have the

G　　　　　　　　**C7**

blues,　　　　　　　ev - 'ry day, ev - 'ry day, ev - 'ry

day, ev - 'ry day I have the blues.

You see

me wor - ry ba - by, 'cause it's you I ____ hate to lose.

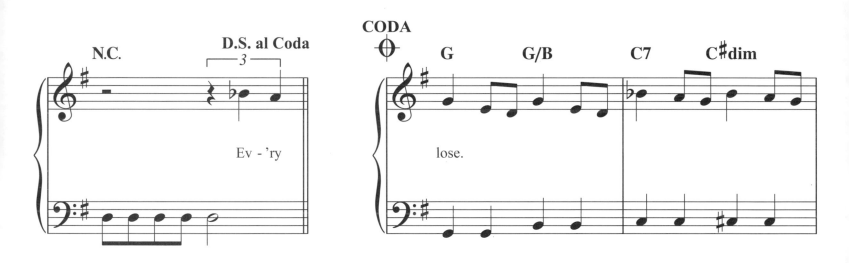

Ev - 'ry

lose.

GEE BABY, AIN'T I GOOD TO YOU

Words by DON REDMAN
and ANDY RAZAF
Music by DON REDMAN

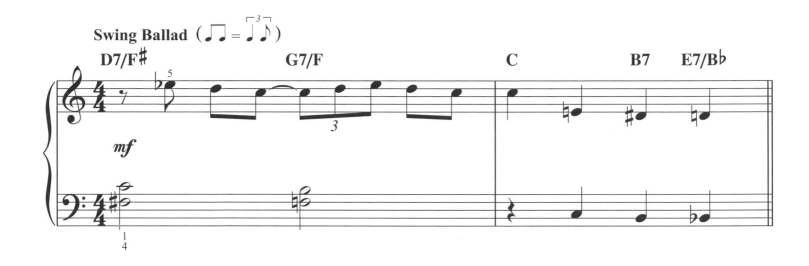

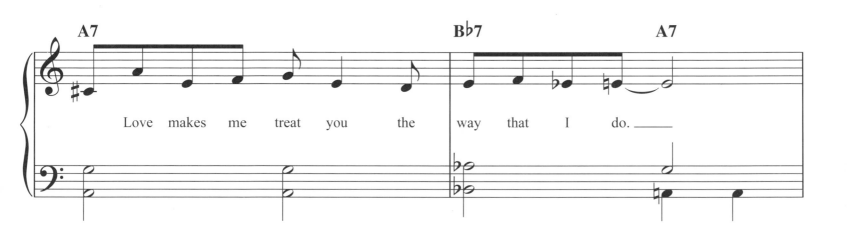

Love makes me treat you the way that I do.

Gee ba - by, _____ ain't I good to you?

There's noth - in' in this world for a girl so sweet and true.

Gee ba - by,____ ain't I ____ good to you.

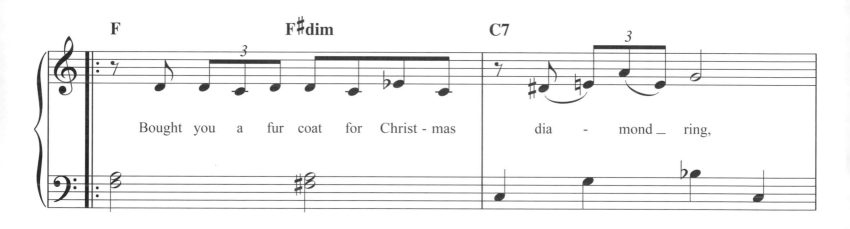

Bought you a fur coat for Christ - mas dia - mond__ ring,

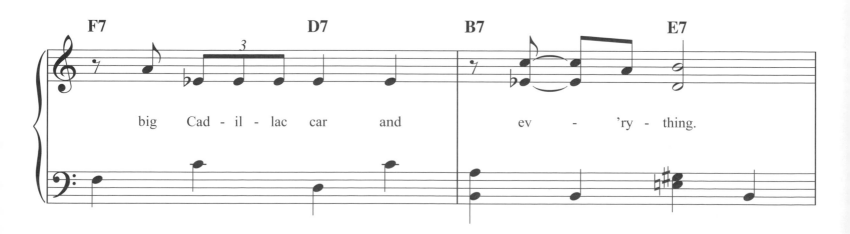

big Cad - il - lac car and ev - 'ry - thing.

What makes me treat you the way that I do? _____

Gee ba - by, _____ ain't I good to you?

1.

Gee ba - by, ain't I good to you.

2.

Gee ba - by, ain't I good to you.

rit.

FEVER

Words and Music by JOHN DAVENPORT
and EDDIE COOLEY

when you kiss me, fe - ver when you hold ___ me tight. Fe - ver in the

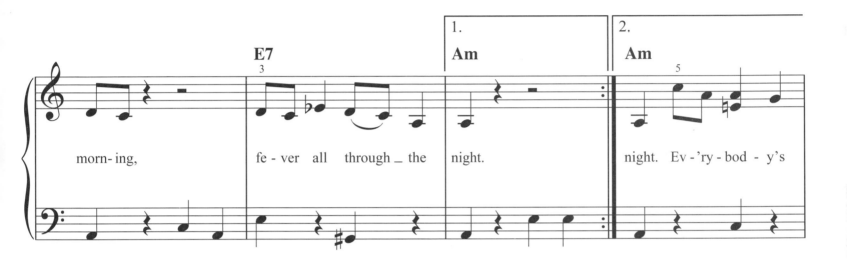

E7   **1. Am**   **2. Am**

morn - ing, fe - ver all through ___ the night. night. Ev - 'ry - bod - y's

got the fe - ver, that is some - thing you all know. Fe - ver is - n't

E7   **Am**

such a new thing. Fe - ver start - ed long ___ a - go.

3. Ro - me - o loved Ju - li - et; ___   Ju - li - et, she felt __ the
4. Cap - tain Smith and Po - ca - han - tas   had a ver - y mad __ af -
5. *(See additional lyrics)*

(L.H. may be played 8va lower to end.)

same.   When he put his arms a - round her,   he said,
fair.   When her dad - dy tried to kill him,   she said,

E7   **Am**

"Ju - lie, ba - by, you're _ my   flame. Thou giv - est fe - ver
"Dad - dy - o, __ don't _ you   dare. He gives me fe - ver

when we kiss - eth,   fe - ver with thy flam - ing   youth.
with his kiss - es,   fe - ver when he holds _ me   tight.

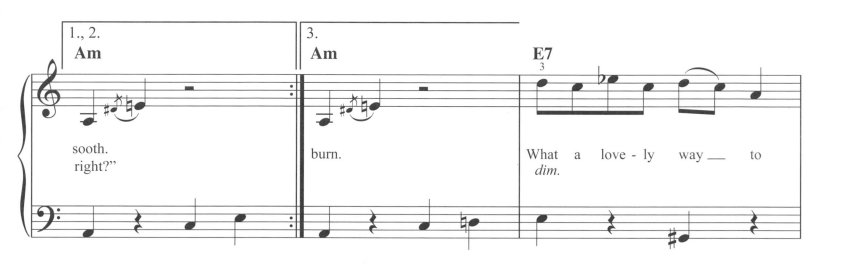

Additional Lyrics

5. Now you've listened to my story.
Here's the point that I have made;
Chicks were born to give you fever,
Be it fahrenheit or centigrade.

They give you fever when you kiss them,
Fever if you live and learn,
Fever! 'Till you sizzle.
What a lovely way to burn.

HELP ME

Words and Music by RALPH BASS,
WILLIE DIXON and WILLIE WILLIAMSON

Moderate Blues

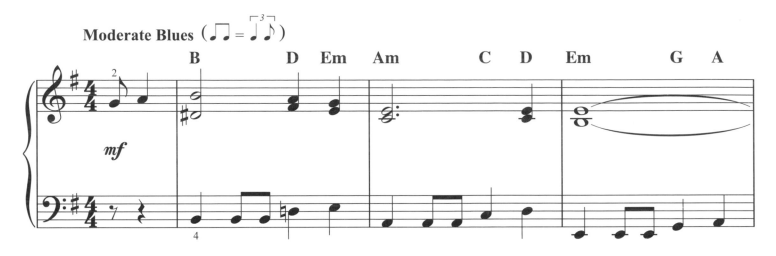

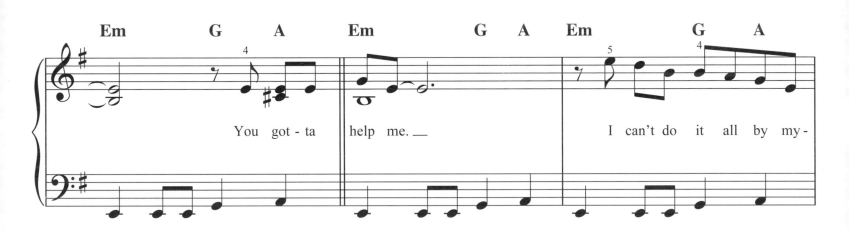

You got-ta help me.___ I can't do it all by my-

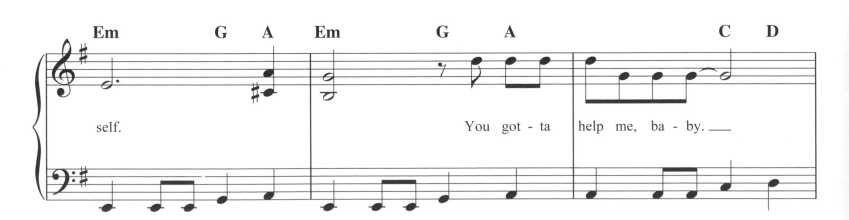

self. You got-ta help me, ba-by.___

I can't do it all by my - self.   You know if you don't

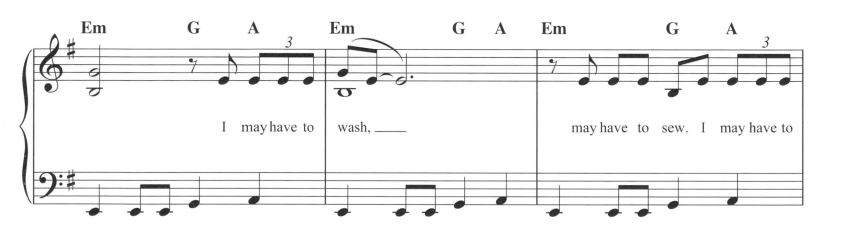

help me, dar - ling, —   I'll have to find my - self some - bod - y else.

I may have to wash, _____   may have to sew. I may have to

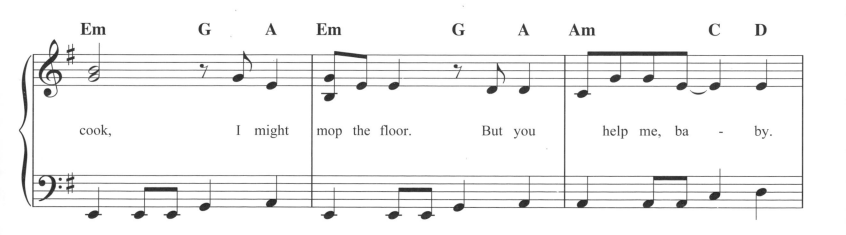

cook,   I might mop the floor.   But you   help me, ba - by.

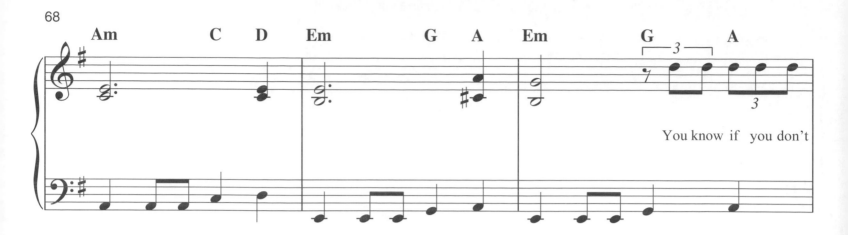

You know if you don't

help me, dar - ling, __   I'll find my - self some-bod - y   else.

When I   walk, _____ you walk with   me.   And when I

talk, __   you talk to   me.   Oh,   babe,

I can't do it all by my-self. You know if you don't

help me, dar-ling, __ I'll have to find my-self some-bod-y else.

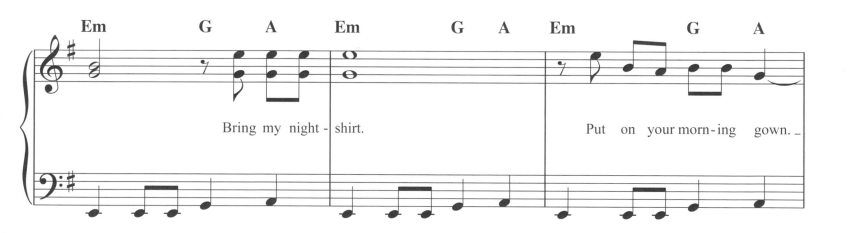

Bring my night-shirt. Put on your morn-ing gown. __

__ Whoa, bring me my night-shirt. __

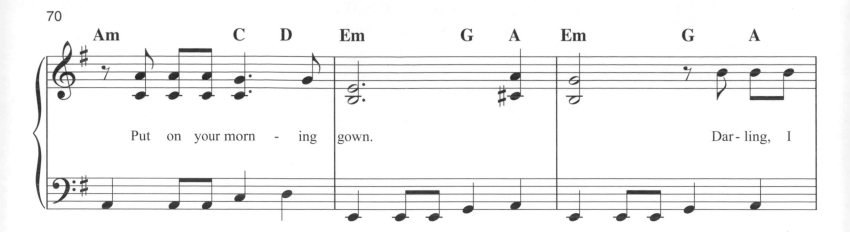

Put on your morn - ing gown. Dar - ling, I

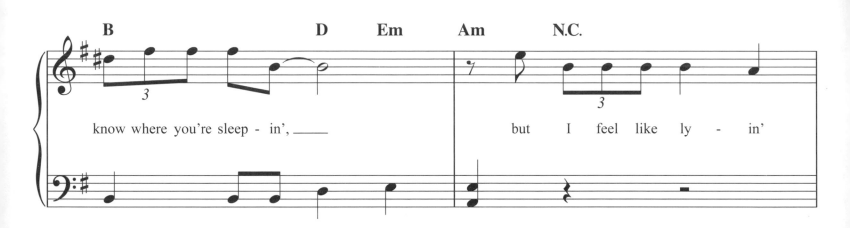

know where you're sleep - in', _____ but I feel like ly - in'

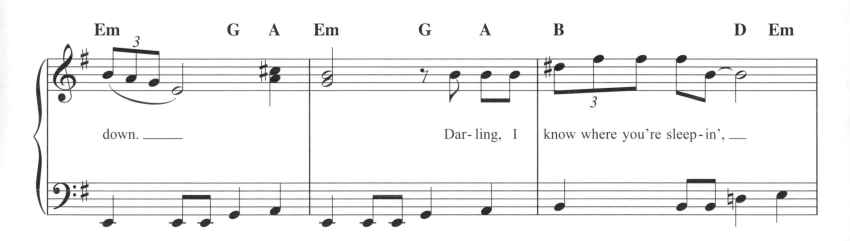

down. _____ Dar - ling, I know where you're sleep-in', ___

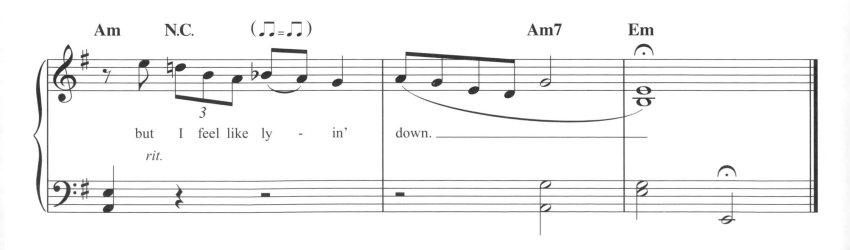

but I feel like ly - in' down. _____

GOT MY MOJO WORKING

Words and Music by
PRESTON FOSTER

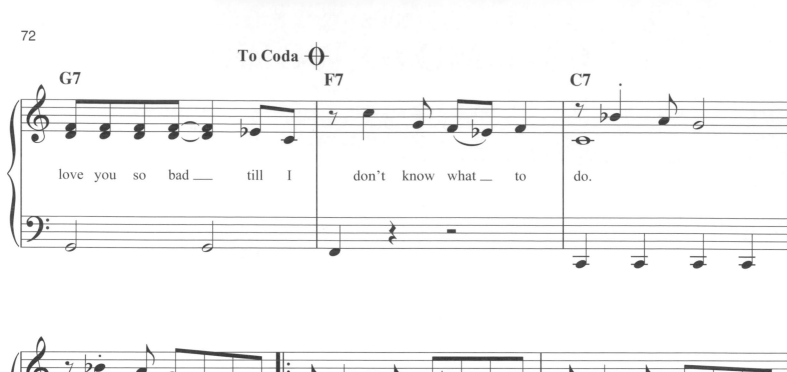

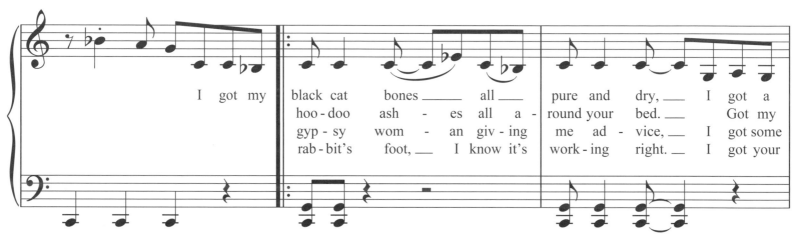

HIDDEN CHARMS

Words and Music by
WILLIE DIXON

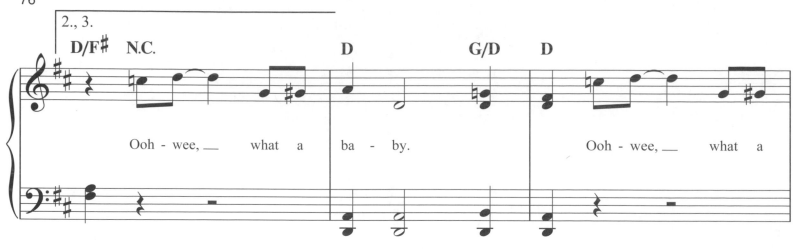

Ooh - wee, ___ what a ba - by. Ooh - wee, ___ what a

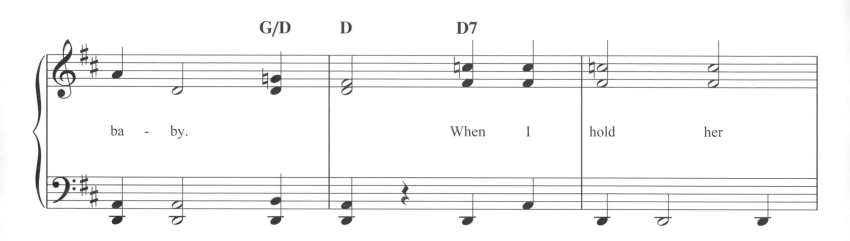

ba - by. When I hold her

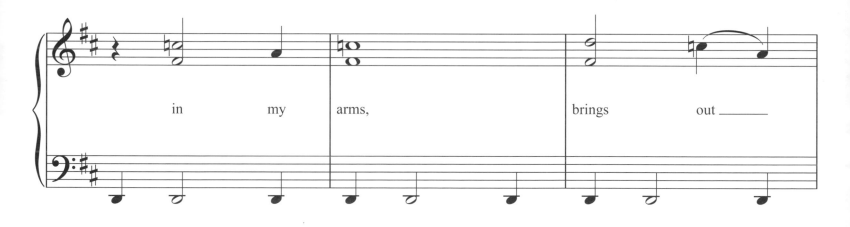

in my arms, brings out ___

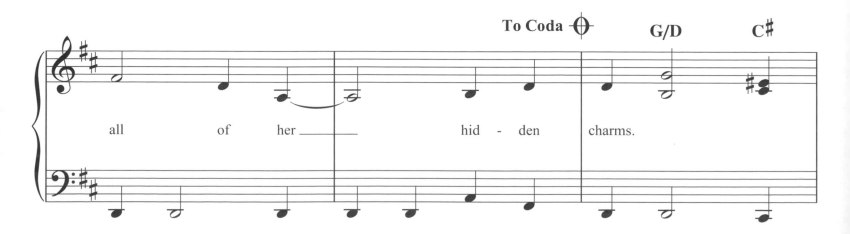

all of her ___ hid - den charms.

D.S. al Coda
(no repeat)

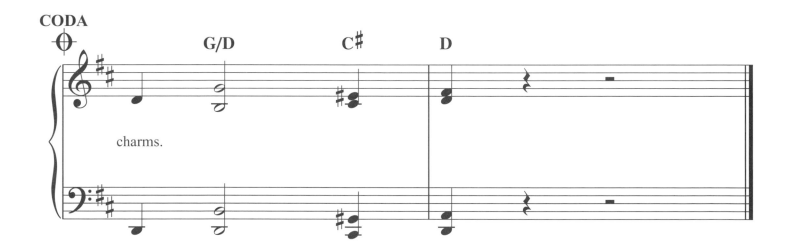

Additional lyrics

2. Her kiss is so pure, as the morning dew.
   Her real gone love, is frantic, too.
   Her eyes, they talk, and say come on.
   What kills me baby is your hidden charms.

3. I told you I love you,
   Stop drivin' me mad.
   When I woke up this morning,
   I never felt so bad.

HOW LONG BLUES
(How Long, How Long Blues)

Words and Music by
LEROY CARR

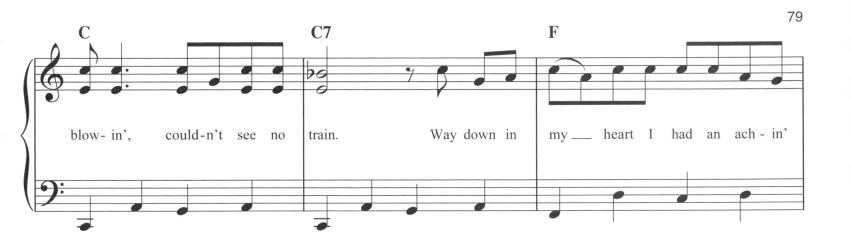

blow- in', could-n't see no train. Way down in my ___ heart I had an ach - in'

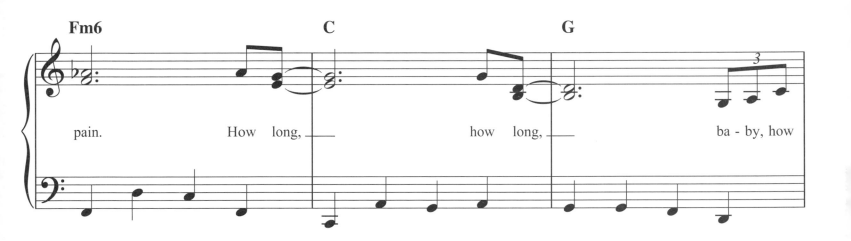

pain. How long, ___ how long, ___ ba - by, how

long? I'm sad and lone - ly all the whole ___ day

through. Why don't you write me and give me the news? You have

Additional Choruses (ad lib.)

If I could holler like a Mountain Jack,
I'd go up the mountain and call my baby back,
How long, how long, how long.

I went up the mountain, looked as far as I could see,
The man (woman) had my woman (man) and the blues had poor me.
How long, how long, how long.

I can see the green grass growing on the hill,
But I ain't seen the green grass on a dollar bill,
For so long, so long, baby so long.

If you don't believe I'm sinkin', see what a hole I'm in.
If you don't believe me, baby, look what a fool I've been,
Well, I'm gone how long, baby, how long.

I'm goin' down to Georgia, been up in Tennessee,
So look me over, baby, the last you'll see of me,
For so long, so long, baby, so long.

The brook runs into the river, the river runs into the sea,
If I don't run into my baby, a train is goin' to run into me,
How long, how long, how long.

I AIN'T GOT YOU

Words and Music by
CALVIN CARTER

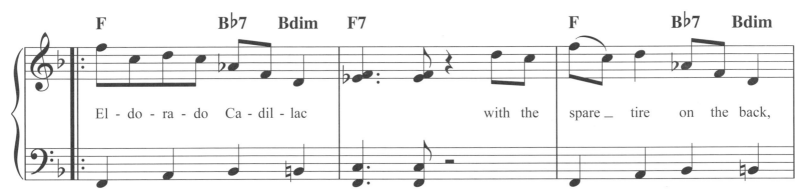

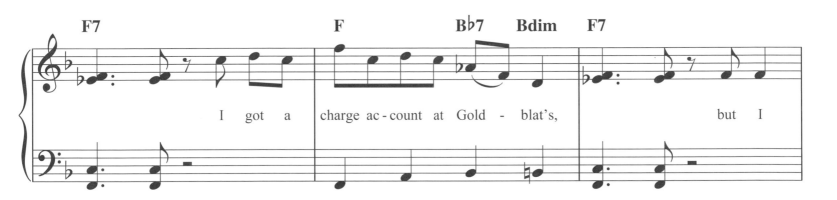

82

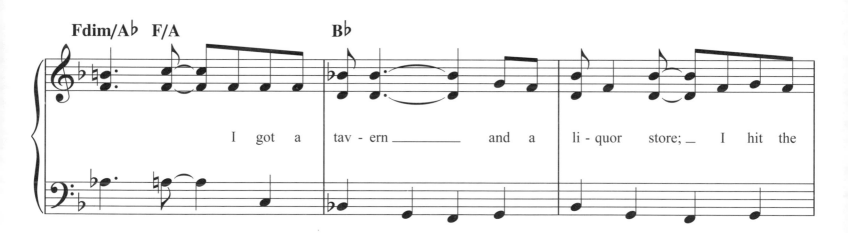

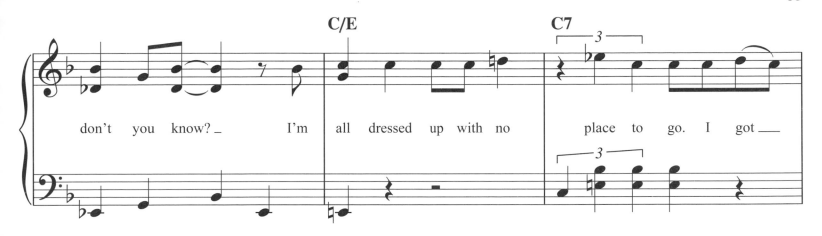

don't you know? _ I'm all dressed up with no place to go. I got ___

wom-en to the left of me, I got ___ wom-en to the right of me,

I got ___ wom-en all a-round _ me but I

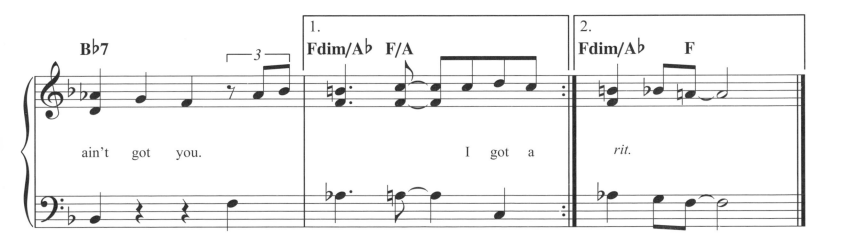

ain't got you. I got a *rit.*

I CAN'T BE SATISFIED

Words and Music by
McKINLEY MORGANFIELD

Medium Country Blues (2 beat feel)

all wor-ried in mind. _____

Well, babe I just can't be sat - is - fied and I

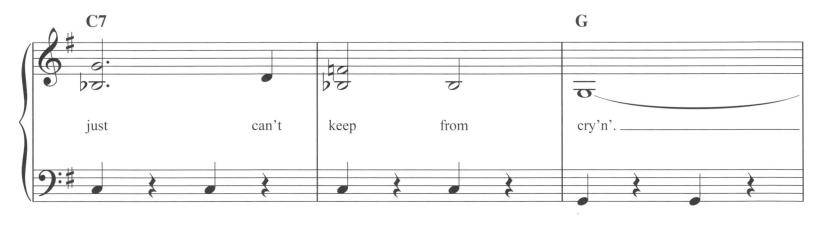

just can't keep from cry'n'. _____

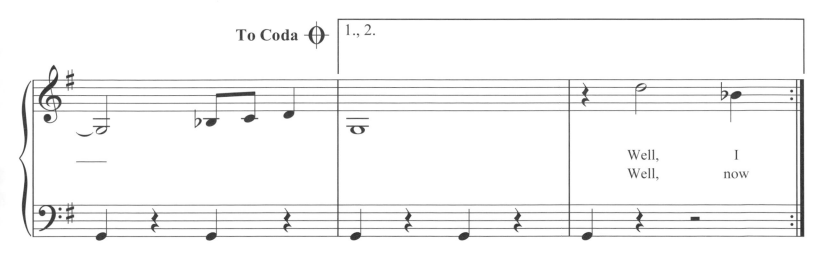

To Coda ⊕ | 1., 2.

_____   Well,   I
        Well,   now

D.S. al Coda

CODA

Well, I

Well, hon - ey,

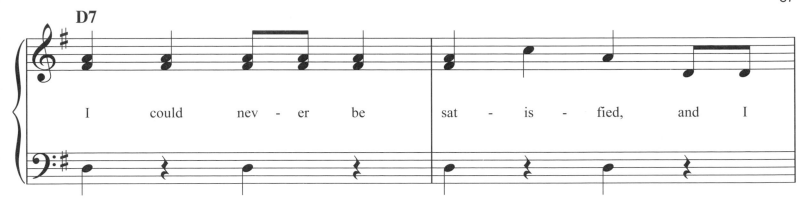

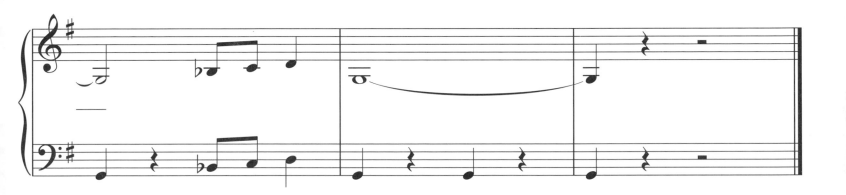

Additional Lyrics

2. Well, I feel like snappin' pistol in your face.
   I'm gonna let some graveyard, Lord, be her restin' place.
   Woman, I'm troubled. I be all worried in mind.
   Well, baby, I can't never be satisfied and I just can't keep from cry'n'.

3. Well, now all in my sleep. Hear my doorbell ring.
   Lookin' for my baby, I didn't see a doggone thing.
   Woman, I was troubled. I was all worried in mind.
   Well, honey, I could never be satisfied, and I just couldn't keep from cry'n'.

4. Well, I know my little old babe. She gonna jump and shout.
   That old train be late, men, Lord, and I come walkin' out.
   I be trouble. I be all worried in mind.
   Well, honey, ain't no way in the world for me to be satisfied, and I just can't keep from cry'n'.

I GOT IT BAD AND THAT AIN'T GOOD

Words by PAUL FRANCIS WEBSTER
Music by DUKE ELLINGTON

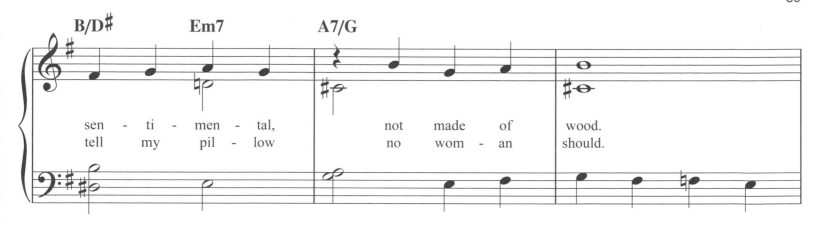

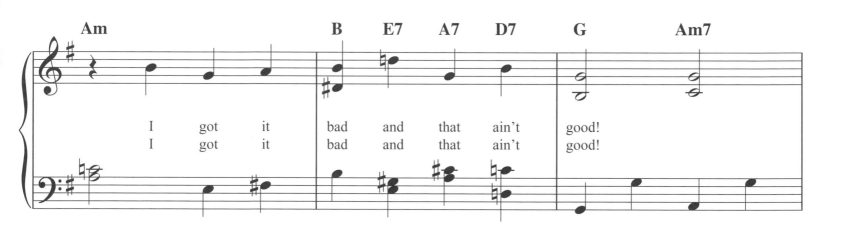

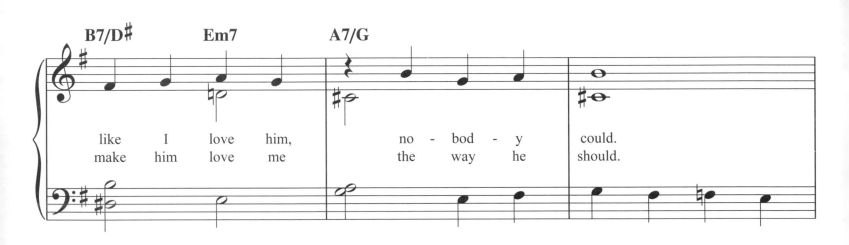

I'D RATHER GO BLIND

Words and Music by ELLINGTON JORDAN
and BILLY POSTER

Some-thing told me ____ it was o - ver ____

when I saw you ____ and her talk - ing. ____

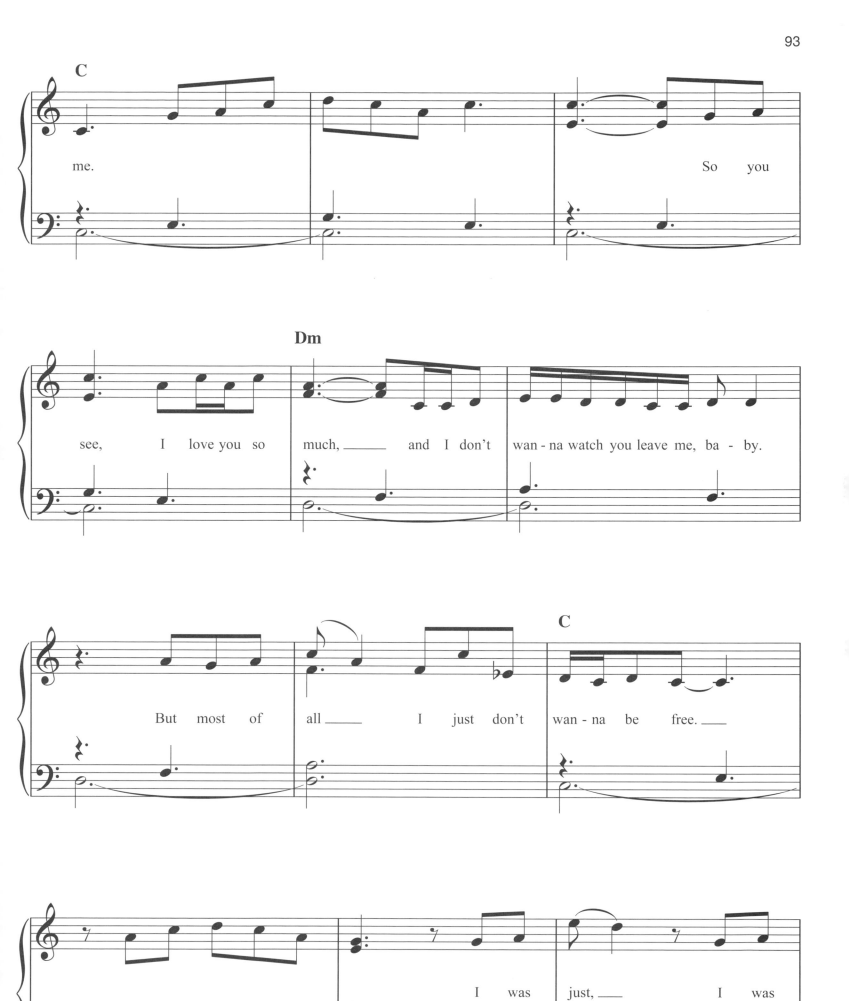

just, ____ I was just ____ sit - ting here think - ing ____ of your

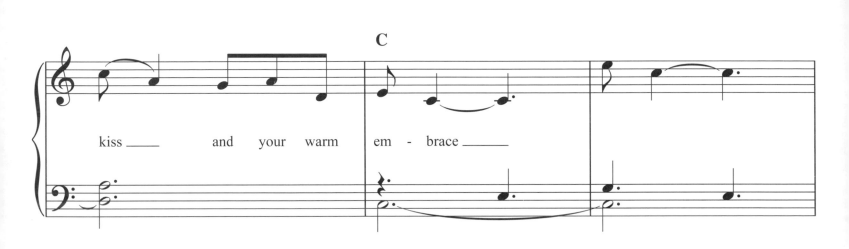

kiss ____ and your warm em - brace ____

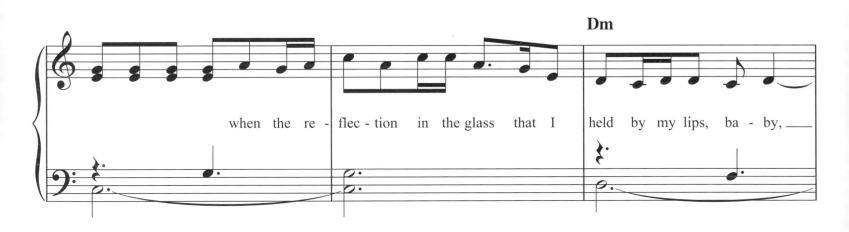

when the re - flec - tion in the glass that I held by my lips, ba - by, ____

____ re - vealed the tears ____ that were on my

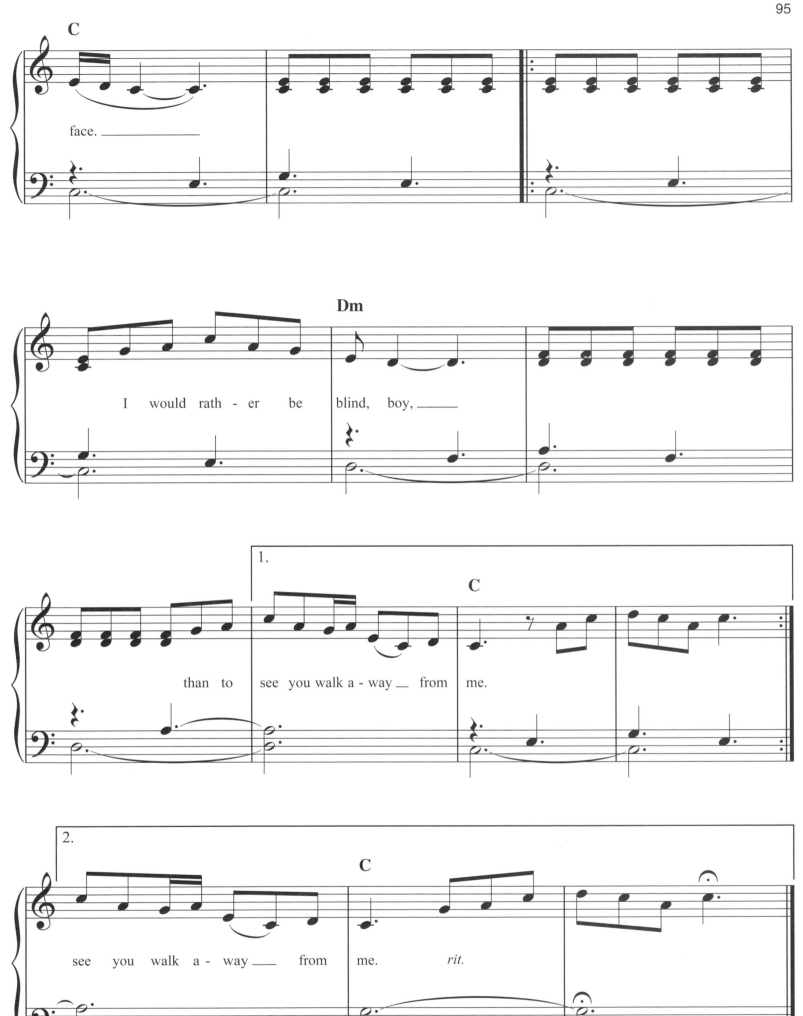

I GOT LOVE IF YOU WANT IT

Words and Music by
JAMES MOORE

Medium Blues (Swing feel)

Got love __ if you want it, babe. Got love __ if you

B♭7/D

want it, babe. Got love __ if you want it.

F7

Got love __ if you want it. Got love __ if you

C7/E   **F7**

want it, we can rock __ all the while,

we can rock ___ all the while.   Quit teas - in' me

babe, ___   quit teas - in' me babe, ___

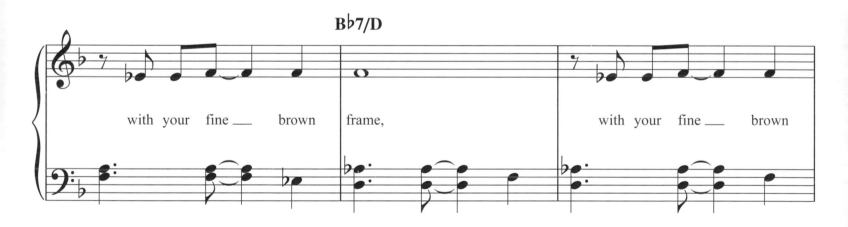

Bb7/D

with your fine ___ brown frame,   with your fine ___ brown

F7   **C7/E**

frame.   If you let ___ me love you, babe,

IS YOU IS, OR IS YOU AIN'T
(Ma' Baby)

Words and Music by BILLY AUSTIN
and LOUIS JORDAN

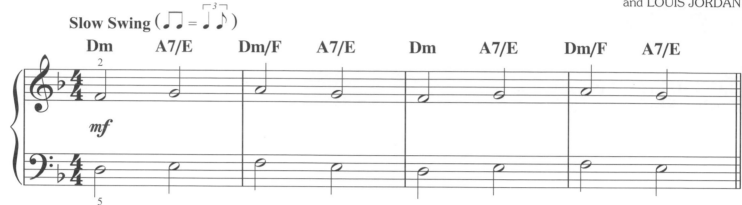

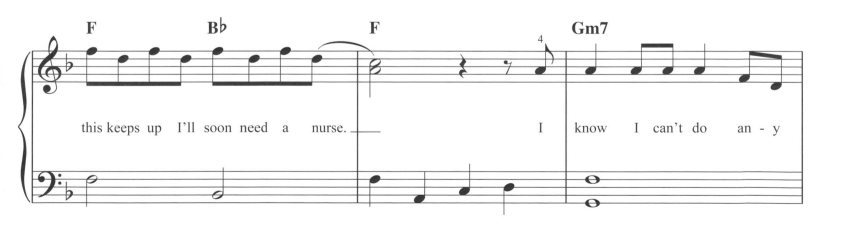

bet - ter, but be - lieve me I could do a lot worse.

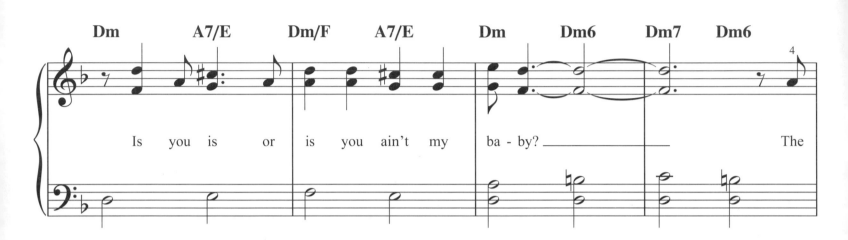

Is you is or is you ain't my ba - by? The

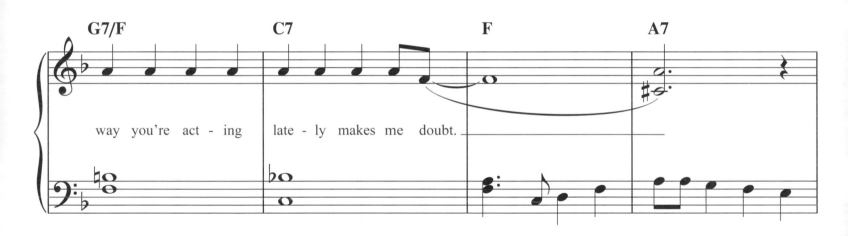

way you're act - ing late - ly makes me doubt.

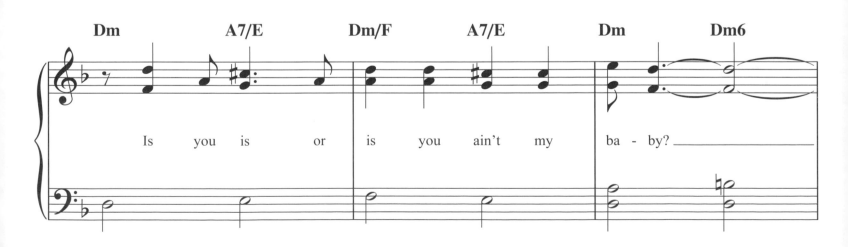

Is you is or is you ain't my ba - by?

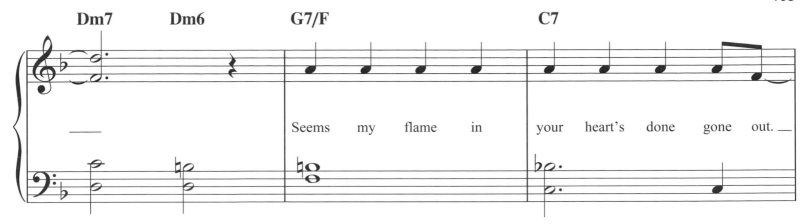

Seems my flame in your heart's done gone out.___

When the moon goes down in the dawn -

- ing and the sun comes up in the morn - ing, don't let the

sun catch you cry - in'. When the moon goes down in the dawn -

- ing,   don't let the   sun catch you cry-in' if your   ba-by don't want __ you no

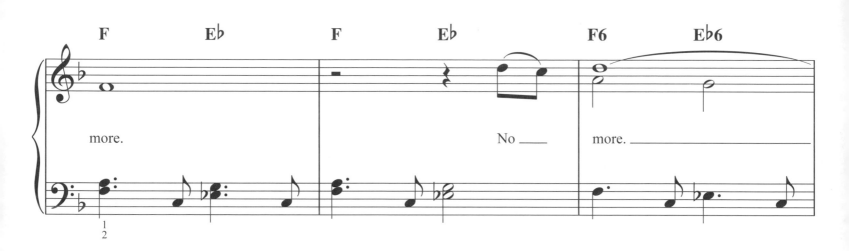

more.   No __ more. __

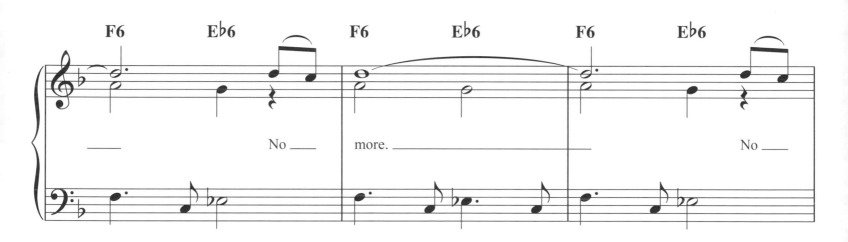

__   No __ more. __   No __

more. __

IT HURTS ME TOO

Words and Music by
MEL LONDON

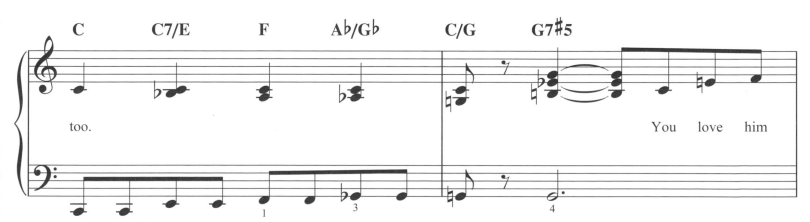

more, _____ when you should love him less, why sneak up be- hind him _____ and you take this

mess. When things go wrong, go wrong with you, it hurts me

too. He loves an-oth-er wom-an and I love

you, but you love him ___ and stick to him like glue. When things go

wrong,　　　　go wrong with　you,　　　it hurts me　too.

He bet-ter　leave you, _____ or you got-ta put him down,　　　be-cause I won't

stay __　to see you pushed a - round.　　When things go　wrong,　　　go wrong with

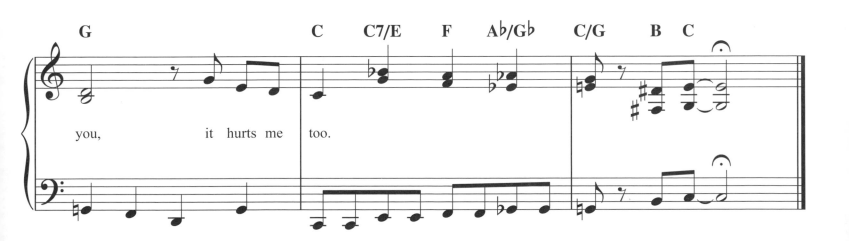

you,　　　it hurts me　too.

KANSAS CITY

Words and Music by JERRY LEIBER
and MIKE STOLLER

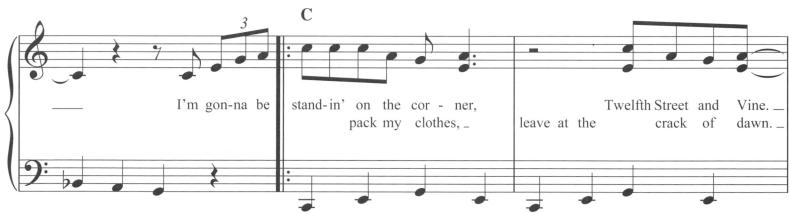

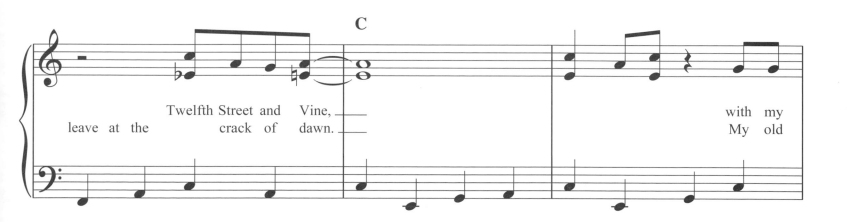

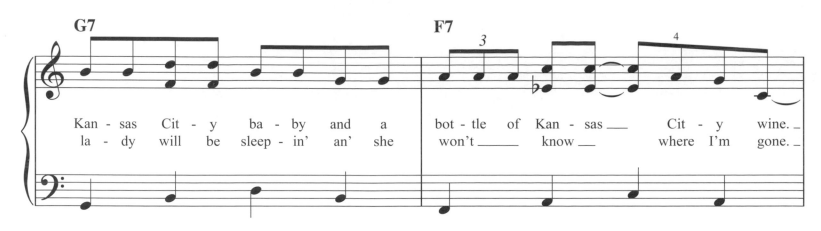

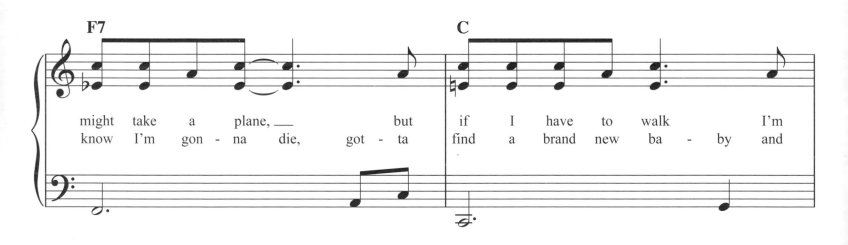

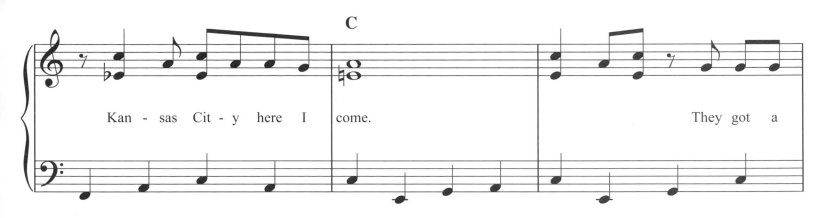

Kan - sas Cit - y here I come. They got a

cra - zy way of lov - in' there and I'm gon - na get me some.

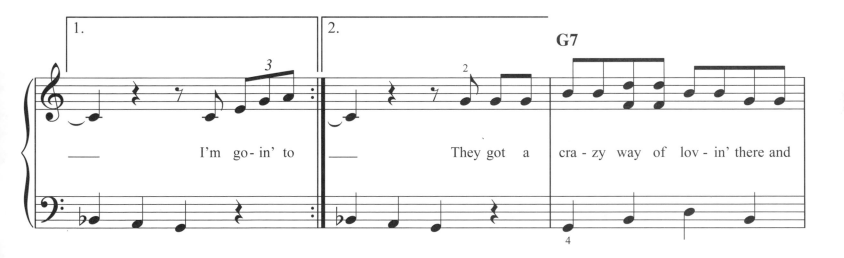

1. I'm go - in' to

2. They got a cra - zy way of lov - in' there and

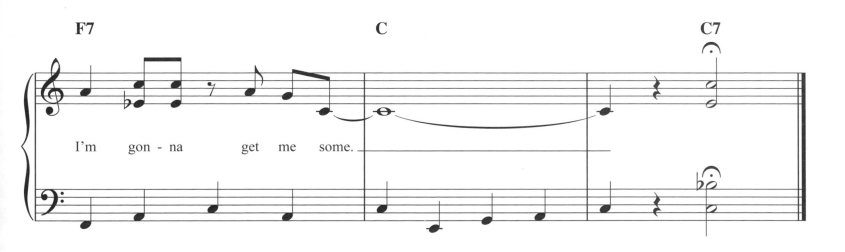

I'm gon - na get me some.

KEY TO THE HIGHWAY

Words and Music by WILLIAM LEE CONLEY BROONZY
and CHAS. SEGAN

Slow Blues

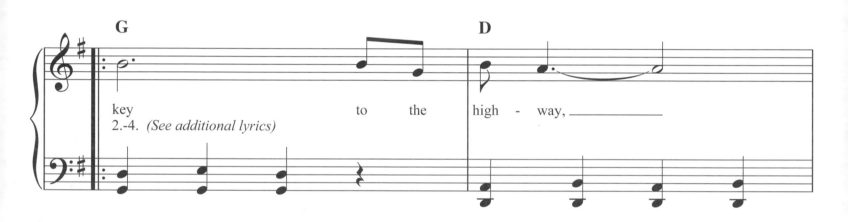

key _____ to the high - way, _____
2.-4. (See additional lyrics)

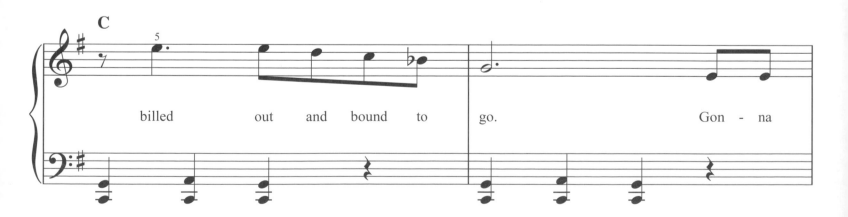

billed out and bound to go. Gon - na

Additional Lyrics

2. I'm goin' back to the border
   Where I'm better known.
   Though you haven't done nothin',
   Drove a good man away from home.

3. Oh, gimmie one more kiss, Mamma,
   Just before I go,
   'Cause when I leave this time,
   I won't be back no more.

4. I got the key to the highway,
   Billed out and bound to go.
   Gonna leave here runnin';
   Walkin' is much too slow.

KIDNEY STEW BLUES

Words and Music by LEONA BLACKMAN
and EDDIE VINSON

Moderate Swing

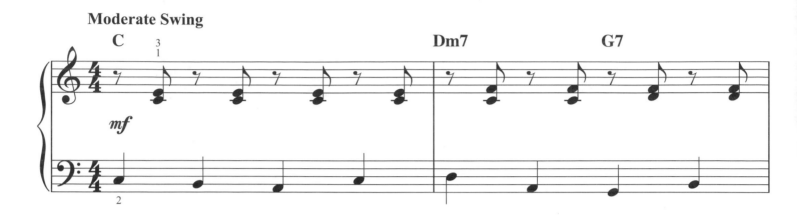

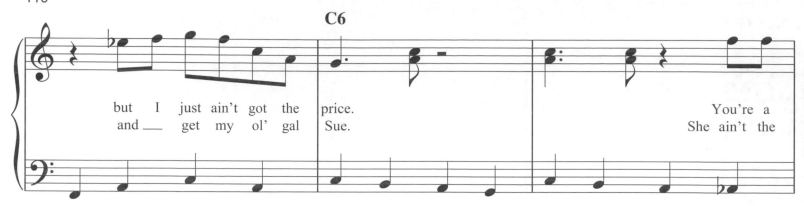

but I just ain't got the price.
and ___ get my ol' gal Sue.

You're a
She ain't the

high - class ma - ma,
cav - i - ar kind,

so I guess it ain't no dice.
just plain ol' kid - ney stew.

Old kid - ney stew, _____ old kid - ney

stew is fine. ___

Old kid - ney stew,

old kid - ney stew is fine. You can

save your mon - ey and keep your peace of

D.S. al Coda

mind.

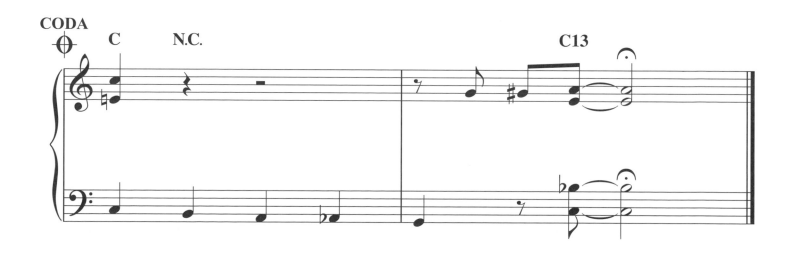

CODA

C   N.C.   C13

LET THE GOOD TIMES ROLL

Words and Music by SAM THEARD
and FLEECIE MOORE

Hey, ev - 'ry - bod - y, let's have some fun. You

on - ly live but once, and when you're dead you're done. ___ Let the

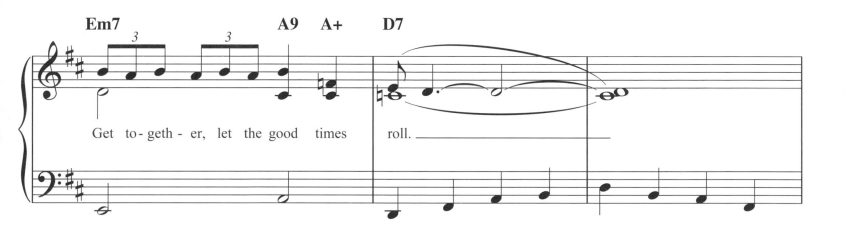

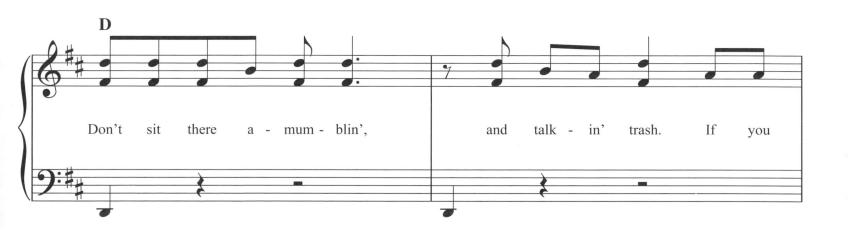

wan - na have a ball you got - ta spend some cash. ___ Let the

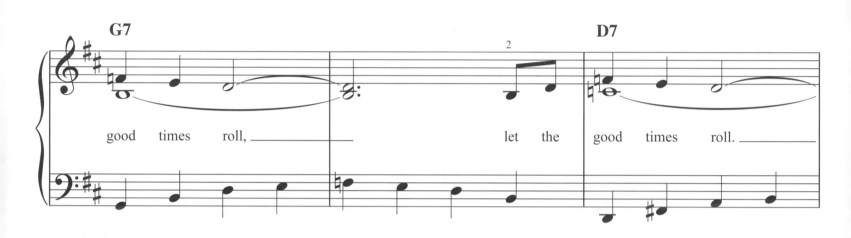

good times roll, ___ ___ let the good times roll. ___

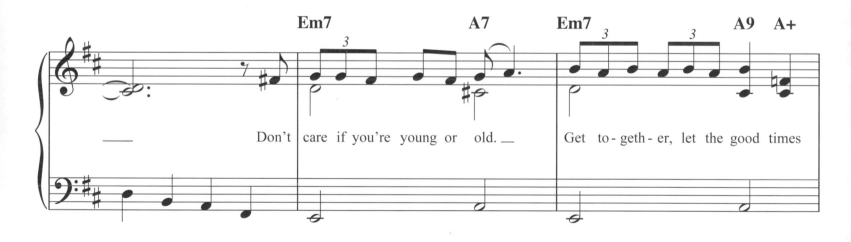

___ Don't care if you're young or old. ___ Get to - geth - er, let the good times

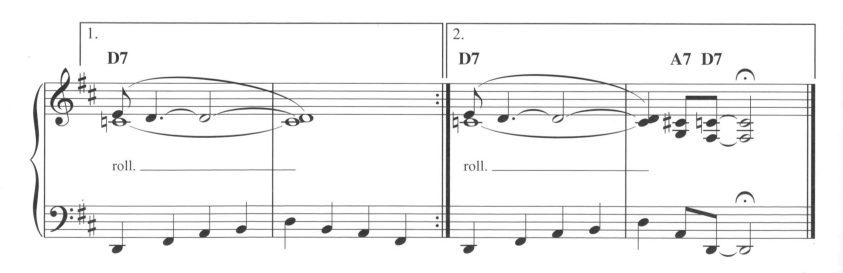

roll. ___

roll. ___

MY BABE

Words and Music by
WILLIE DIXON

Oh, yes, I know she loves me, she don't do noth-in' but

kiss and hug me. My babe, true lit-tle ba-by is

my babe. my babe, true lit-tle ba-by is

my babe. True lit-tle ba-by is my babe.

NIGHT TRAIN

Words by OSCAR WASHINGTON
and LEWIS C. SIMPKINS
Music by JIMMY FORREST

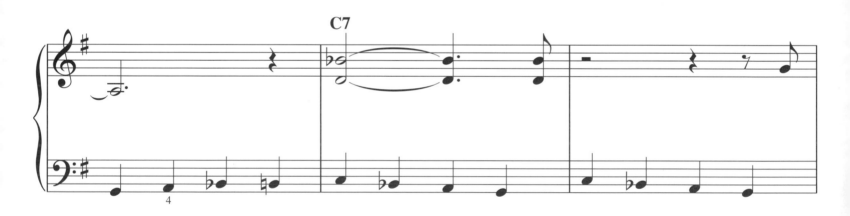

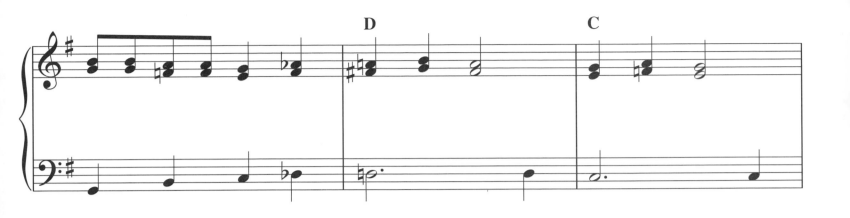

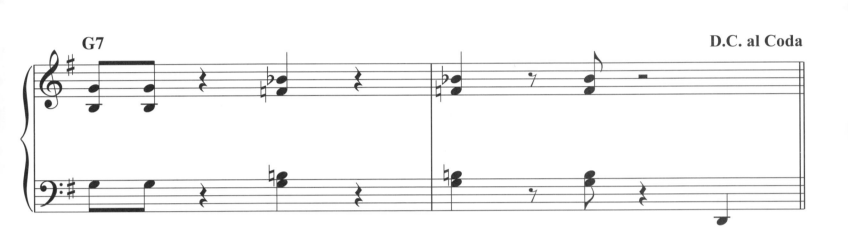

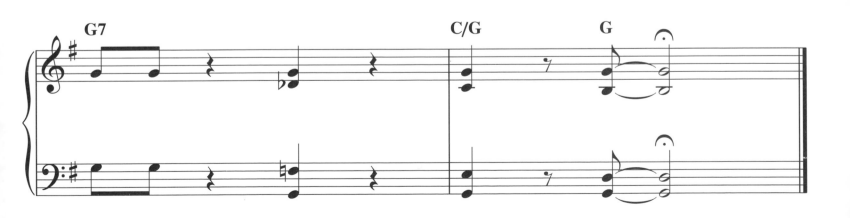

ROUTE 66

By BOBBY TROUP

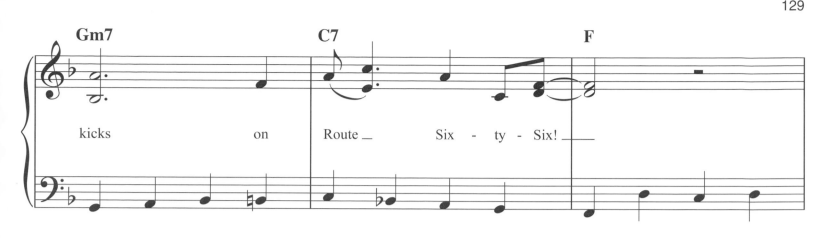

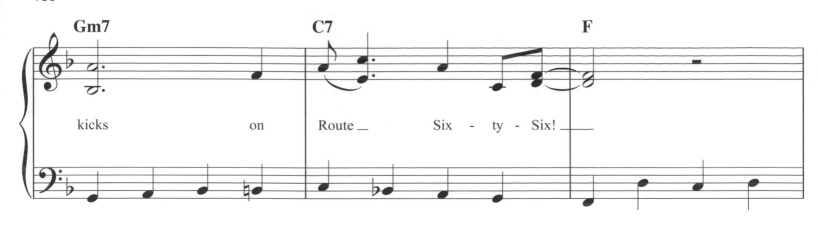

Gm7   **C7**   **F**

kicks   on   Route   Six - ty - Six!

F7   **C7**   **F7**   **Bb7/F**

Now you   go   thru Saint Loo - ey,   Jop - lin, Mis - sou - ri   and

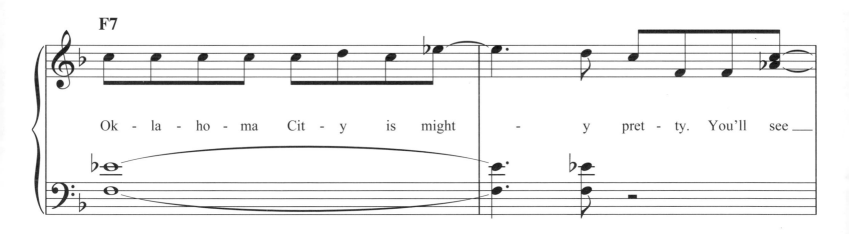

F7

Ok - la - ho - ma Cit - y is might   -   y pret - ty. You'll see ___

Bb7   **F**

___   Am - ar - il - lo, ___   Gal - lup, New

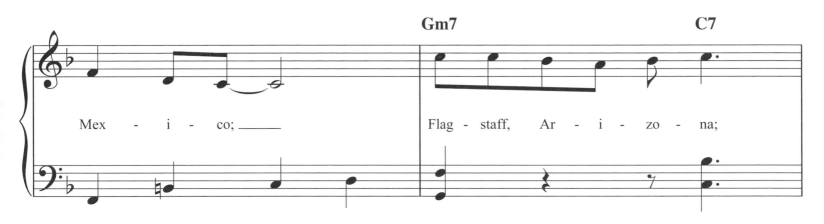

Mex - i - co; _____ Flag - staff, Ar - i - zo - na;

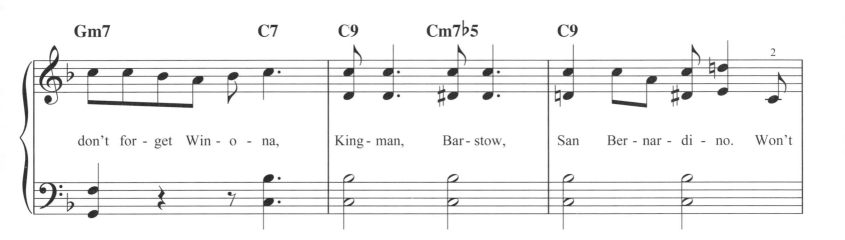

don't for - get Win - o - na, King - man, Bar - stow, San Ber - nar - di - no. Won't

you _____ get hip to this time - ly tip _____

when you _____ make that Cal - i - for - nia trip. _____

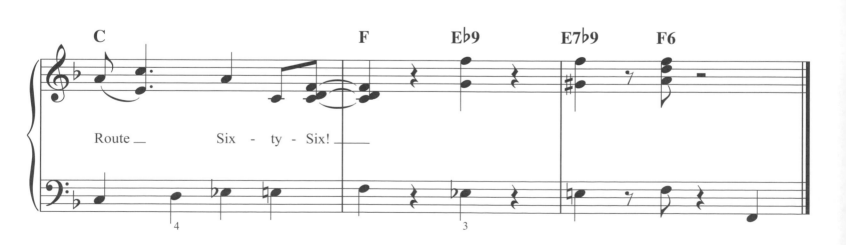

NOBODY KNOWS YOU WHEN YOU'RE DOWN AND OUT

(Nobody Knows When You're Down And Out)

Words and Music by
JIMMIE COX

place I'd go.___ If I ev-er get my hands on a dol-lar a-gain,___ I'm gon-na

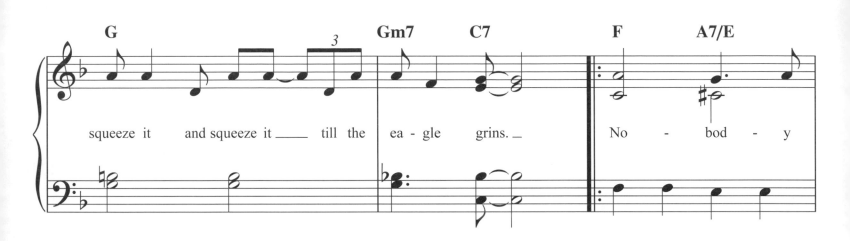

squeeze it and squeeze it ___ till the ea-gle grins. ___ No - bod - y

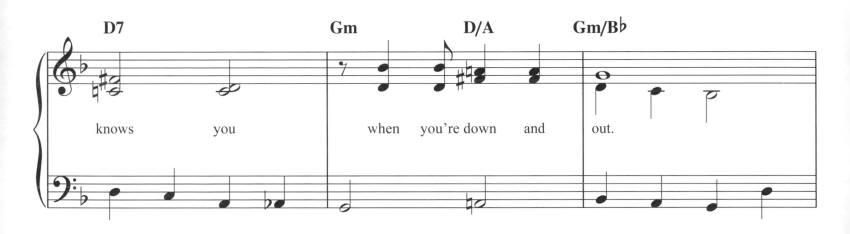

knows you when you're down and out.

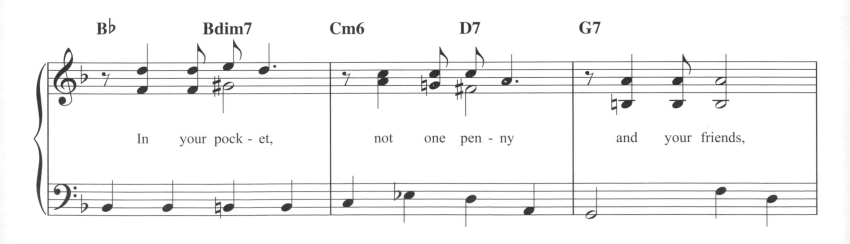

In your pock - et, not one pen - ny and your friends,

SAINT JAMES INFIRMARY

Words and Music by
JOE PRIMROSE

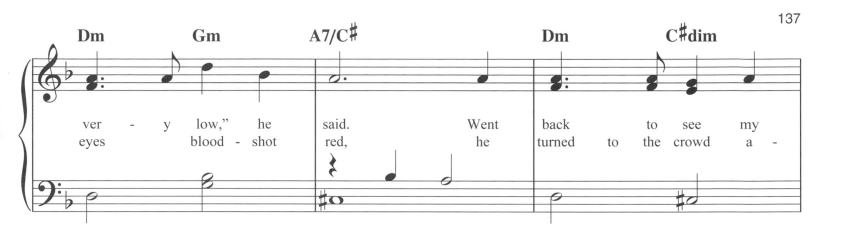

Dm ... **Gm** ... **A7/C♯** ... **Dm** ... **C♯dim**

ver - y low," he said. Went back to see my
eyes blood - shot red, he turned to the crowd a -

Dm/C ... **Bm7♭5** ... **B♭7** ... **A7** ... *1.* **Dm**

ba - by; great __ God! she was ly - in' there dead. I went
round him, these __ are the __ words __ he

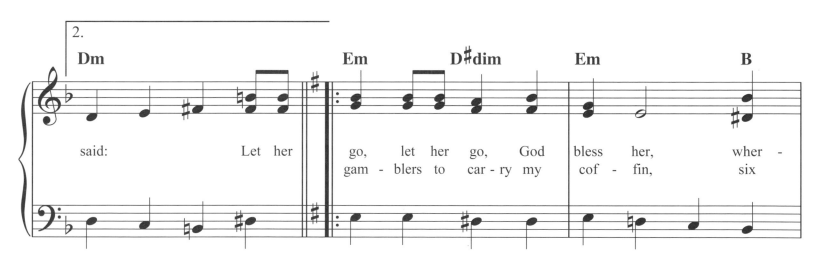

2. **Dm** ... **Em** ... **D♯dim** ... **Em** ... **B**

said: Let her go, let her go, God bless her, wher -
gam - blers to car - ry my cof - fin, six

Em ... **Am** ... **B** ... **Em** ... **D♯dim**

ev - er she may be; she may search this wide world
cho - rus girls to sing my song; put a jazz band on my

o - ver, she'll nev - er find a man like me. Oh,
tail gate to raise hell as we go a - long. Now

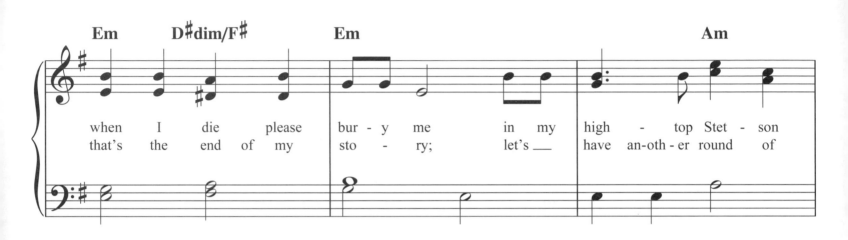

when I die please bur - y me in my high - top Stet - son
that's the end of my sto - ry; let's have an-oth-er round of

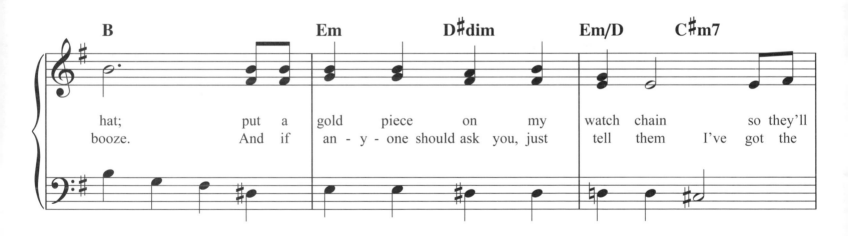

hat; put a gold piece on my watch chain so they'll
booze. And if an - y - one should ask you, just tell them I've got the

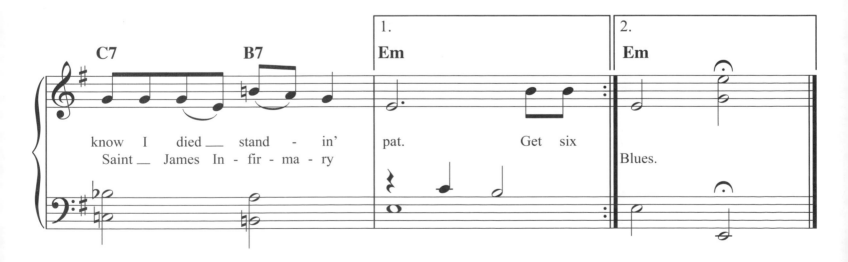

know I died stand - in' pat. Get six
Saint James In - fir - ma - ry Blues.

PLEASE ACCEPT MY LOVE

Words and Music by B.B. KING
and SAUL BIHARI

PRIDE AND JOY

Words and Music by
STEVIE RAY VAUGHN

pride and joy. ___ She's my sweet lit - tle ba - by,

1.

I'm her ___ lit - tle lov - er boy. Yeah. I

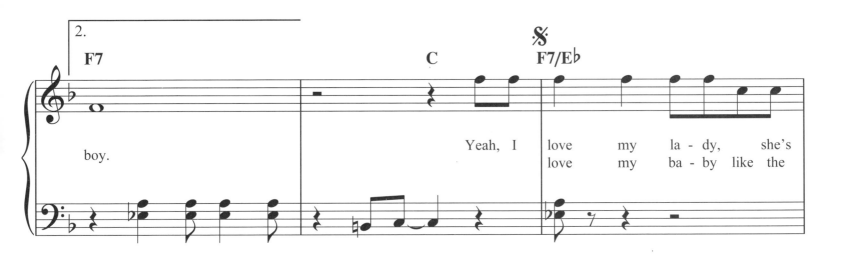

2.

boy. Yeah, I love my la - dy, she's
love my ba - by like the

long and ___ lean. ___ You mess with her, you'll see a man get mean. ___
fin - est ___ wine. ___ Stick with her ___ un - til the end of time. ___ } Yes, she's my

sweet lit - tle thing. ____ She's my pride and joy. ____

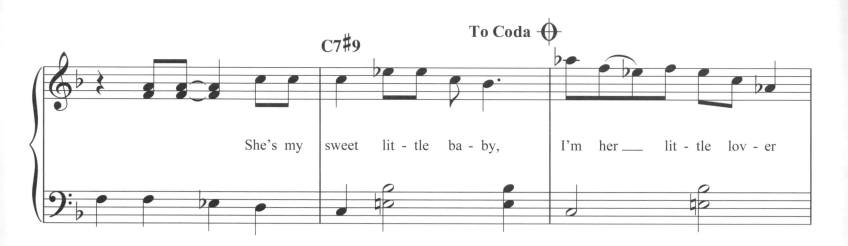

She's my sweet lit - tle ba - by, I'm her ___ lit - tle lov - er

boy.

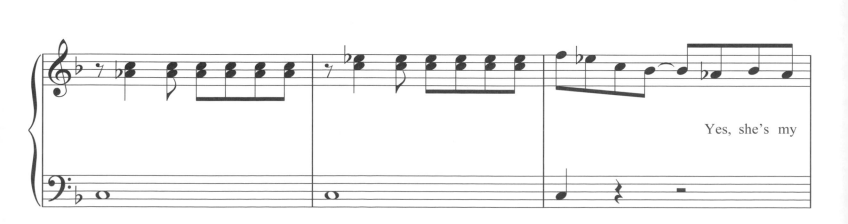

Yes, she's my

sweet lit - tle thing. _____ She's my pride and joy. ___

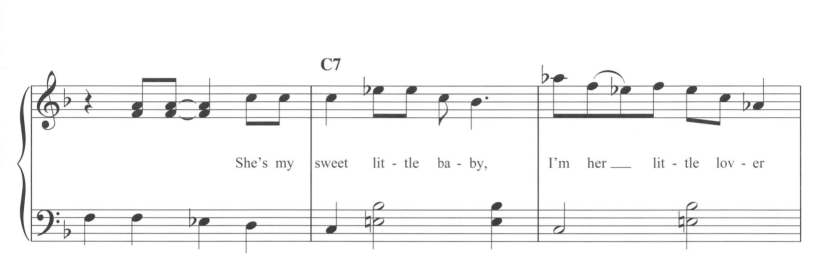

She's my sweet lit - tle ba - by, I'm her __ lit - tle lov - er

boy. Yeah, I

I'm her __ lit - tle lov - er

boy.

ST. LOUIS BLUES

from BIRTH OF THE BLUES

Words and Music by
W.C. HANDY

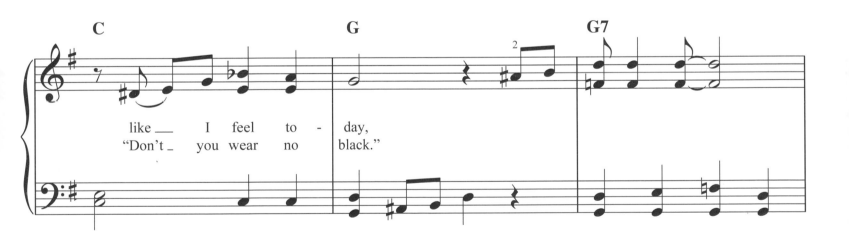

148

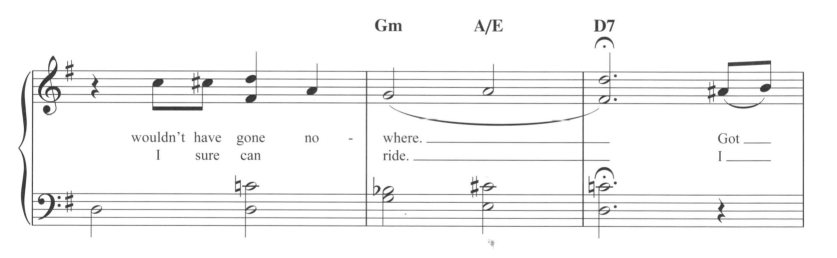
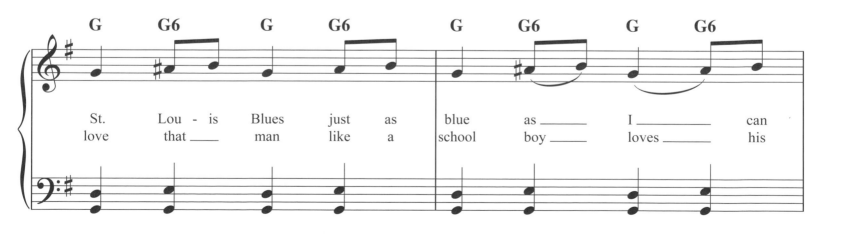

SEE SEE RIDER

Words and Music by
MA RAINEY

made me love — you. Now your gal has come.

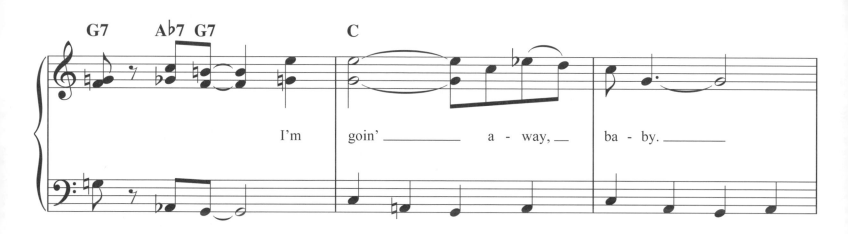

I'm goin' _____ a - way, — ba - by. _____

I won't be back 'til fall. — Law'd, Law'd, Law'd, goin' a - way, ba - by.

Won't be back 'til fall. If I

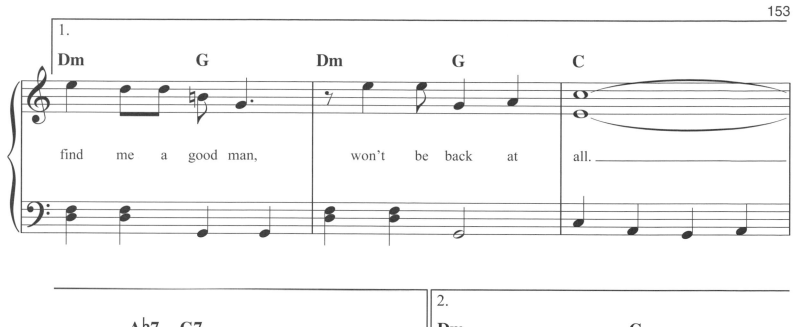

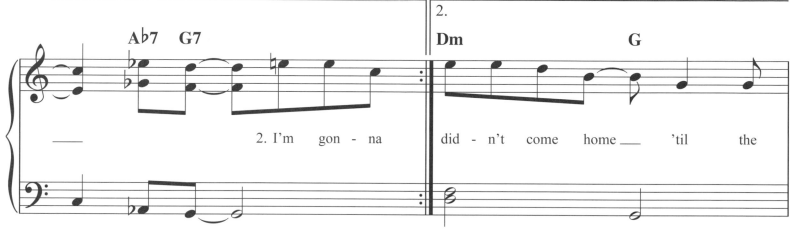

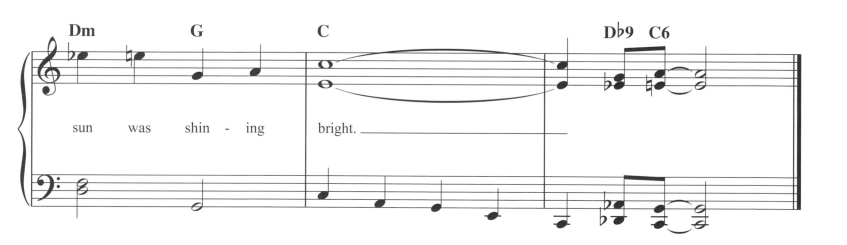

Additional Lyrics

2. I'm gonna buy me a pistol just as long as I am tall.
   Law'd, Law'd, Law'd, shoot my man and catch a cannonball.
   If he won't have me, he won't have no gal at all.
   See See Rider, where did you stay last night?
   Law'd, Law'd, Law'd, your shoes ain't buttoned, your clothes don't fit you right.
   You didn't come home 'til the sun was shining bright.

SITTING ON TOP OF THE WORLD

Words and Music by
CHESTER BURNETT

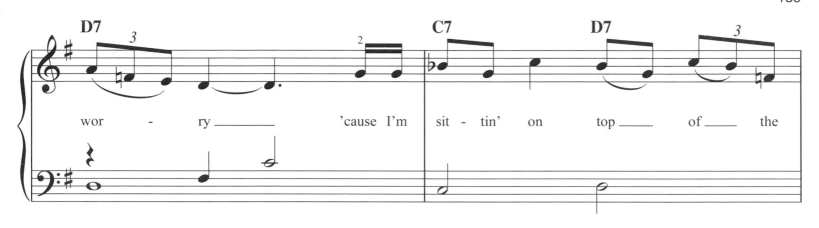

wor - ry _____ 'cause I'm sit - tin' on top ___ of ___ the

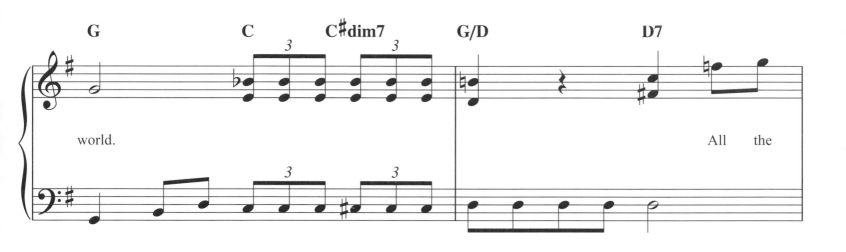

world. All the

sum - mer _____ worked on this farm _____ had to take

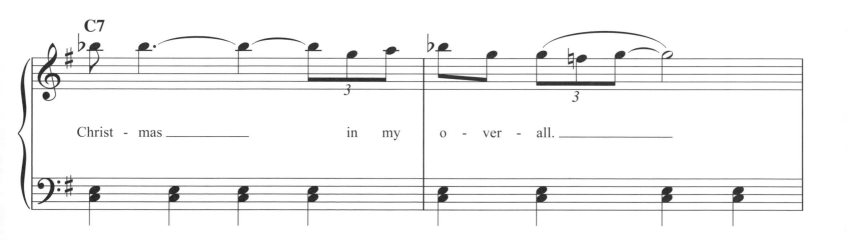

Christ - mas _____ in my o - ver - all. _____

She's gone, but I don't_____ wor - ry _____ 'cause I'm

sit - tin' on top _____ of _____ the world.

One sum-mer don't _____ wor - ry _____ 'cause I'm

sit - tin', sit - tin' on top of the world. _____

molto rall.

STORMY WEATHER
(Keeps Rainin' All the Time)
from COTTON CLUB PARADE OF 1933

Words by TED KOEHLER
Music by HAROLD ARLEN

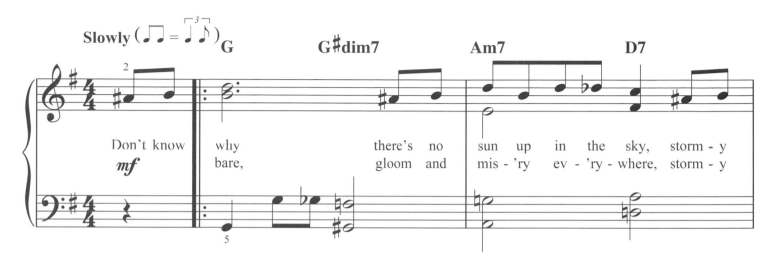

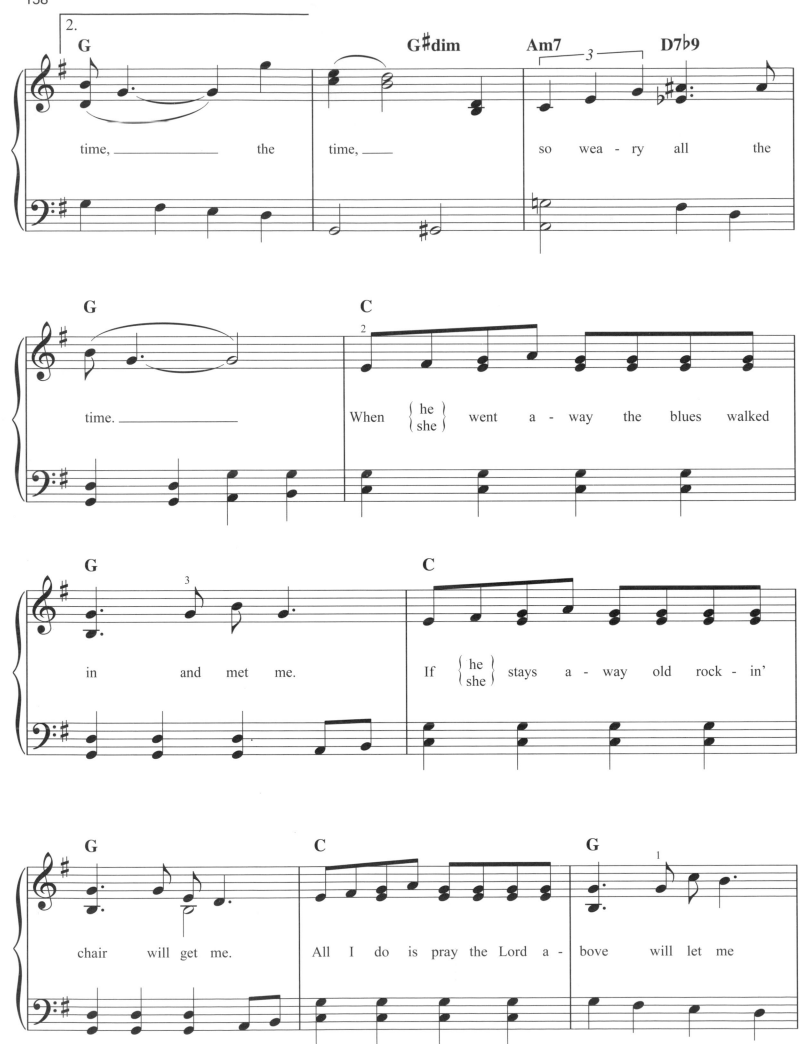

159

(They Call It)
STORMY MONDAY
(Stormy Monday Blues)

Words and Music by
AARON "T-BONE" WALKER

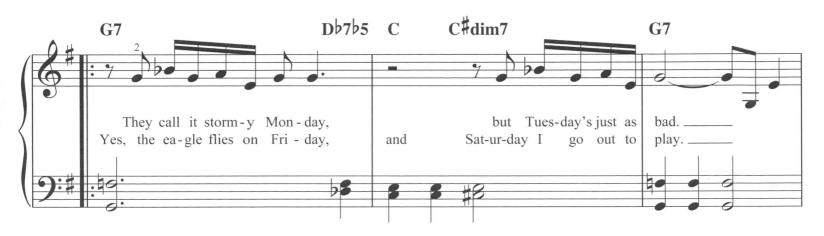

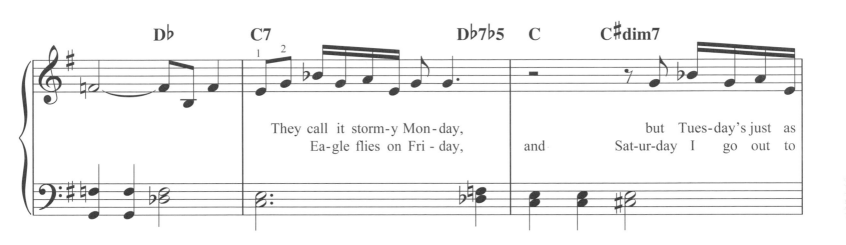

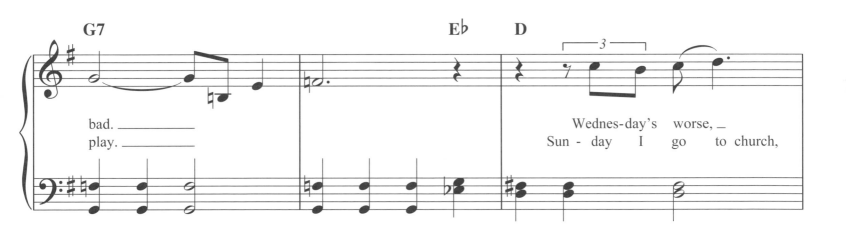

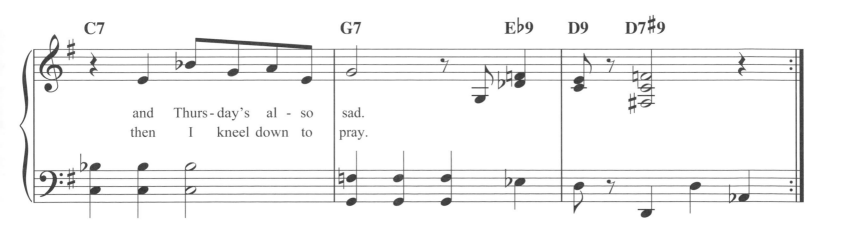

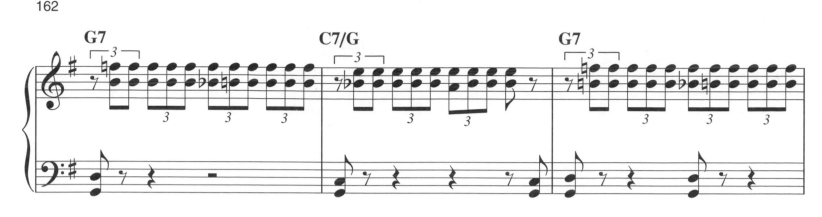

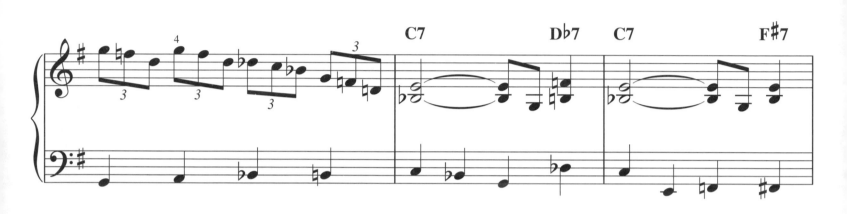

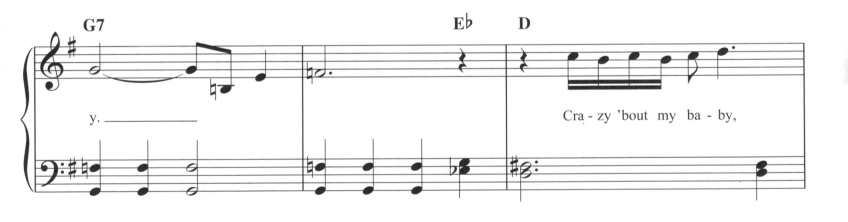

TANQUERAY

Words and Music by JOHNNIE JOHNSON
and KEITH RICHARDS

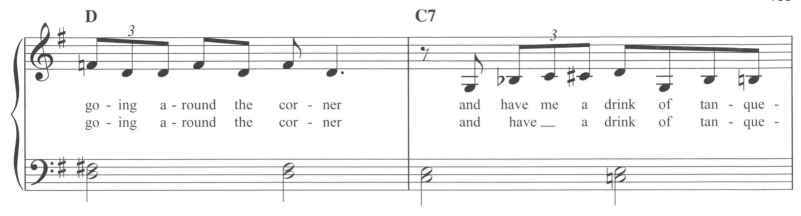

go - ing a - round the cor - ner and have me a drink of tan - que -
go - ing a - round the cor - ner and have __ a drink of tan - que -

ray.
ray.
It was a

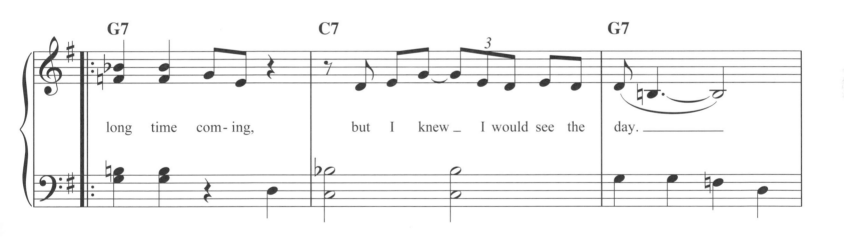

long time com - ing, but I knew __ I would see the day. _____

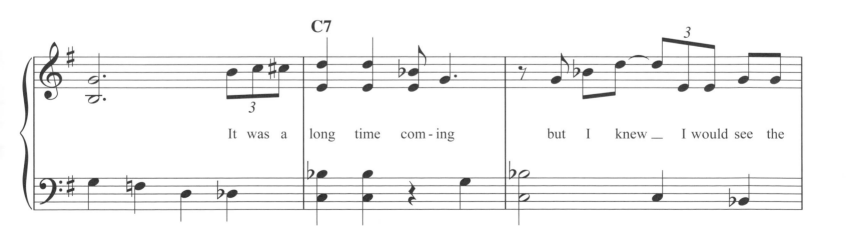

It was a long time com - ing but I knew __ I would see the

day _____ when you and I could sit down __ and

have a drink of tan - que - ray. _____ It was a

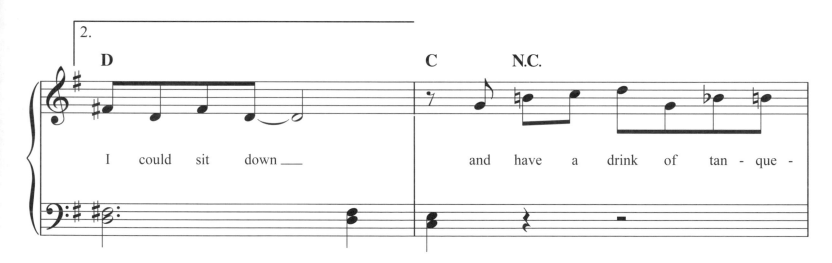

I could sit down ___ and have a drink of tan - que -

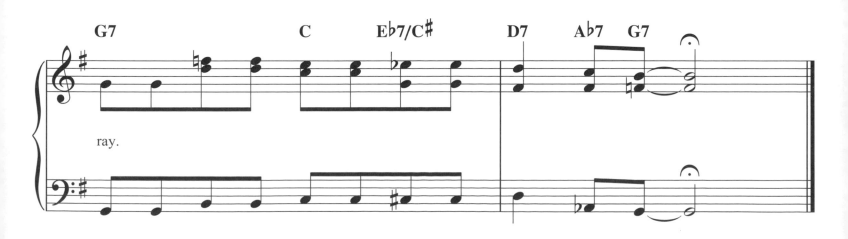

ray.

A SUNDAY KIND OF LOVE

Words and Music by LOUIS PRIMA,
ANITA NYE, STANLEY RHODES
and BARBARA BELLE

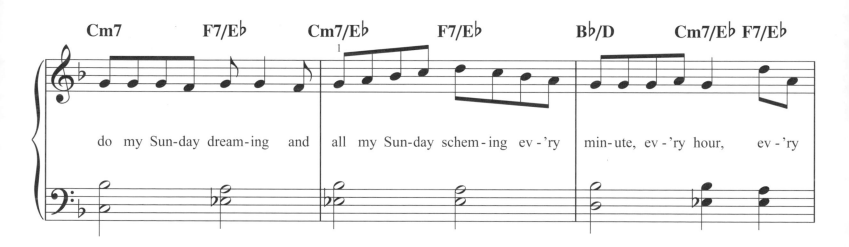

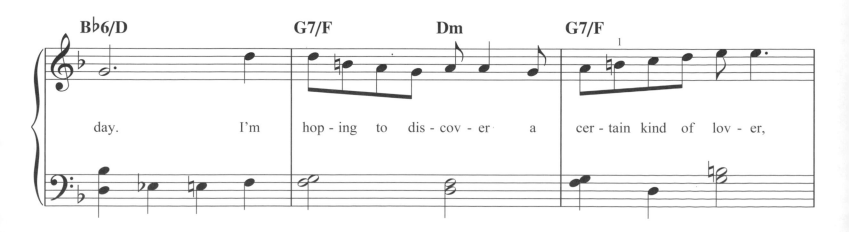

who will show me the way. My arms need some-one to en-fold, __

to keep me warm when Mon-days are cold, __ a love for all my life to

have and to hold. __ I want a Sun-day kind of love.

I want a love. *rit.*

SWEET HOME CHICAGO

Words and Music by
ROBERT JOHNSON

same old ___ place, ___   sweet home ___ Chi - ca - go. ___

1.   2., 3.

Come

Well, _ one and one is two, ___
Well, _ six and three is nine, ___

six and two is eight. _   Come on, ___ ba - by, don't-cha   make me late! _
nine and nine is eight-een.   Look there, broth - er, ba - by, have you seen   what I've seen? _

Hey,   ba - by, don't-cha wan - na   go ___

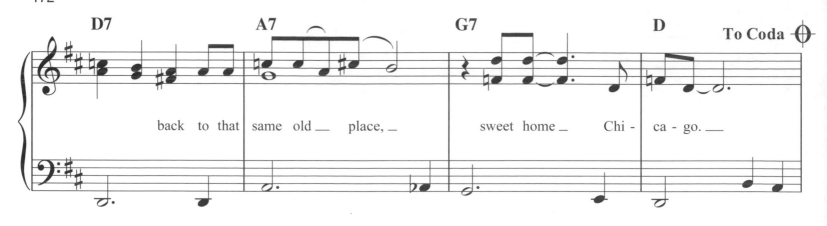

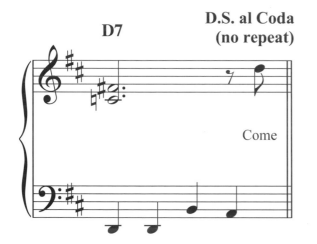

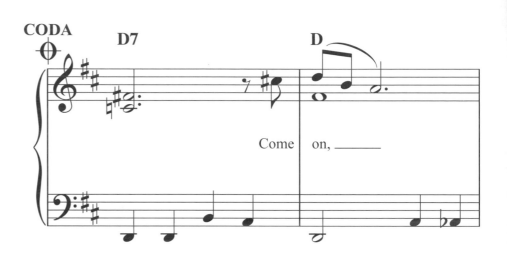

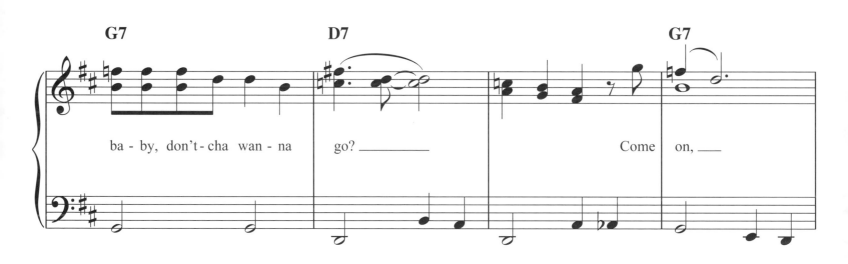

same old ___ place, ___ my sweet home Chi - ca go. ___

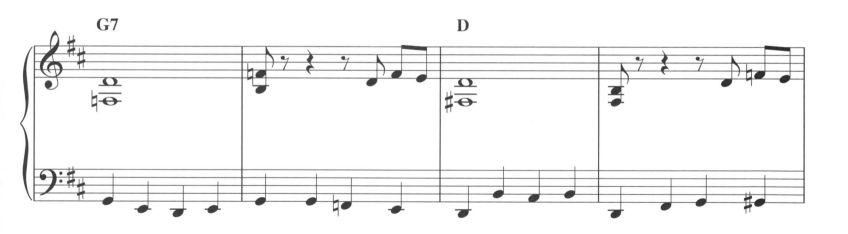

THINGS AIN'T WHAT THEY USED TO BE

Words and Music by
MERCER ELLINGTON

175

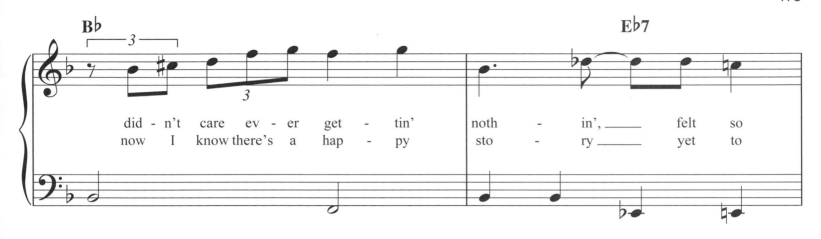

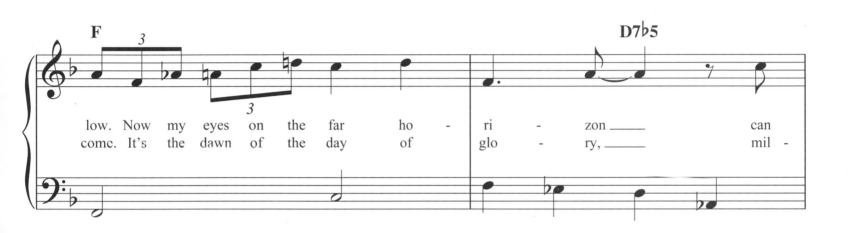

To Coda ⊕

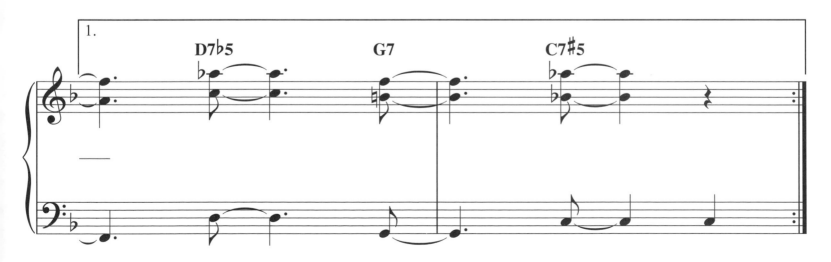

Look at that

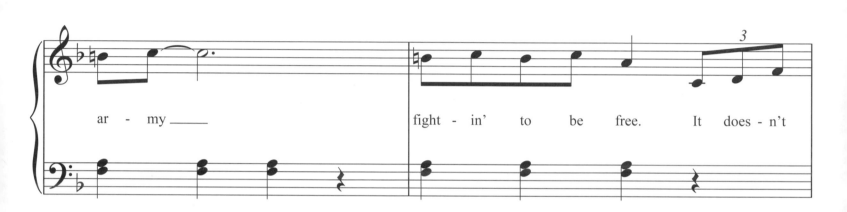

ar - my _____ fight - in' to be free. It does - n't

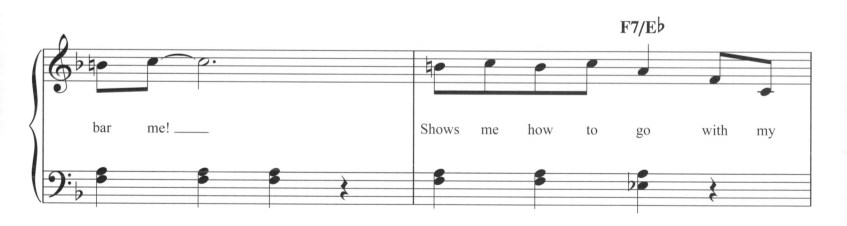

bar me! _____ Shows me how to go with my

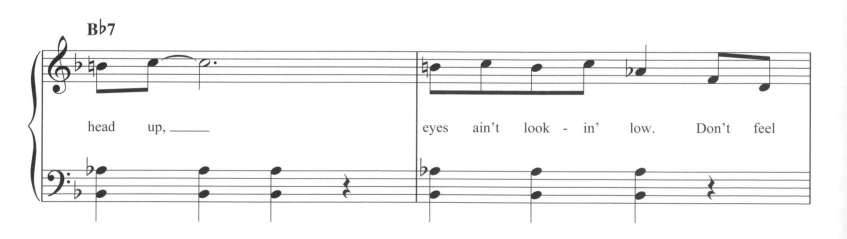

head up, _____ eyes ain't look - in' low. Don't feel

fed up, _____ that's how come I see a

vic - to - ry; _____ be - lieve me things ain't what they used to be. ___

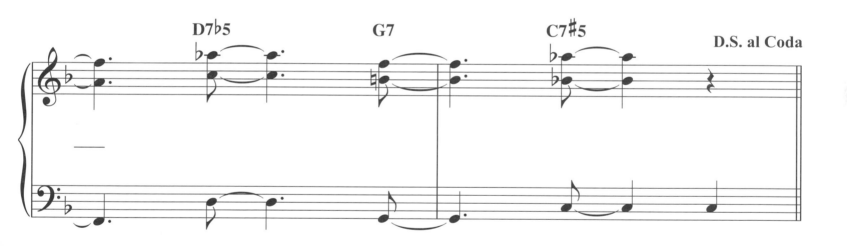

D.S. al Coda

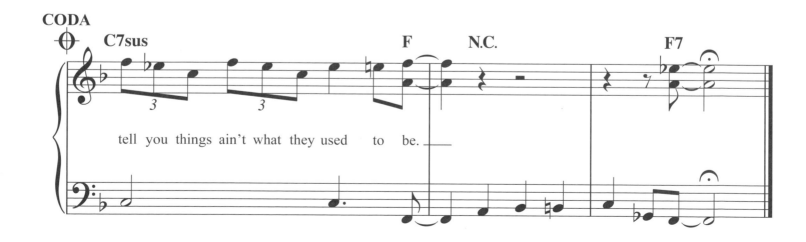

tell you things ain't what they used to be. ___

WEST END BLUES

Words and Music by JOE OLIVER
and CLARENCE WILLIAMS

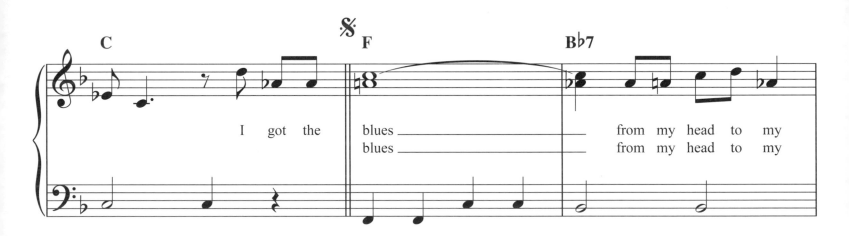

I got the blues _____ from my head to my
blues _____ from my head to my

shoes. _____ I'm blue to-day. I've got _ a mean _ e-vil feel-in'.
shoes. _____ Blue to-day. I've got _ a mean _ low-down feel-in'.

To Coda ⊕

My bel-ly's full ___ of gin. ___ I'm on ___ my
I'm gon-na hear ___ bad news. ___ I'm on ___ my

way to the West End and that's where trou-bles will be - gin.

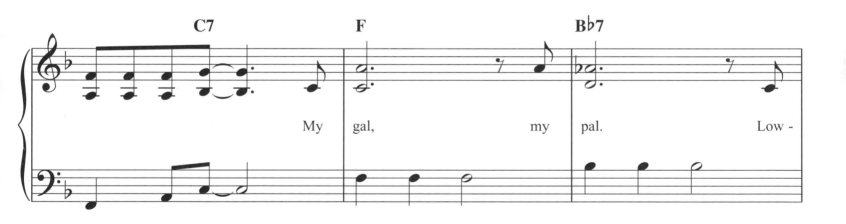

My gal, my pal. Low -

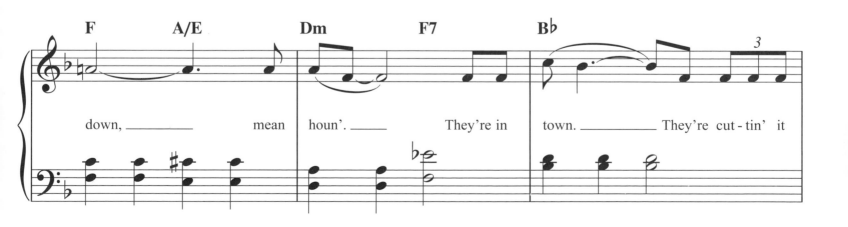

down, ___ mean houn'. ___ They're in town. ___ They're cut-tin' it

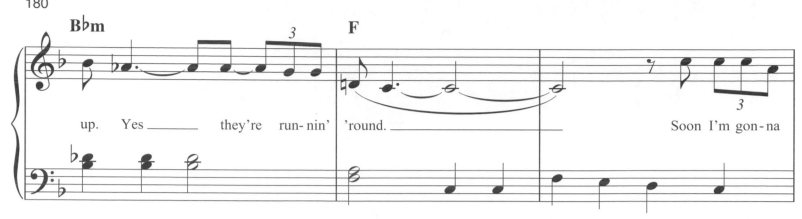

up. Yes ____ they're run-nin' 'round. _____ Soon I'm gon-na

take a walk ____ and knock up - on ____ her door.

Now those ____ folks _____ in West End, _____

folks _____ in West End they're gon - na see ____ some shoot- in' like

they nev - er saw be - fore. _____ My

gal and my __ best pal ____ will nev - er cheat in West End an - y -

more. _ I got the

way to the West End to

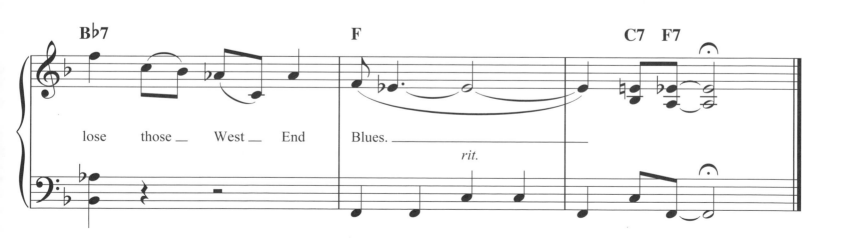

lose those __ West __ End Blues. _____

I got the way to the West End to

THE THRILL IS GONE

Words and Music by ROY HAWKINS
and RICK DARNELL

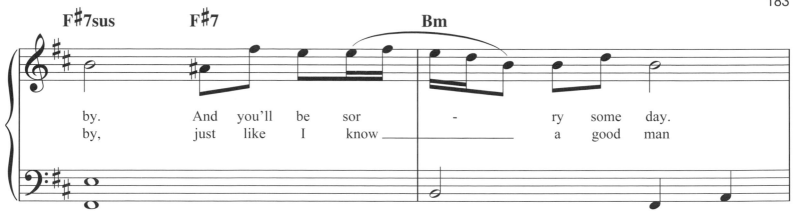

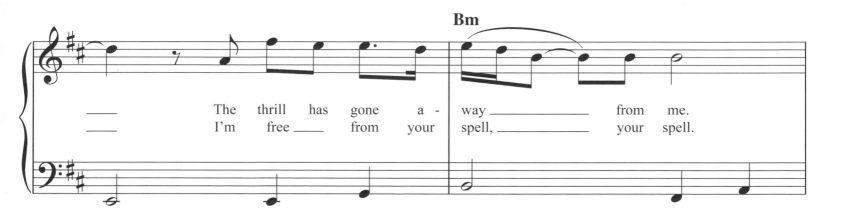

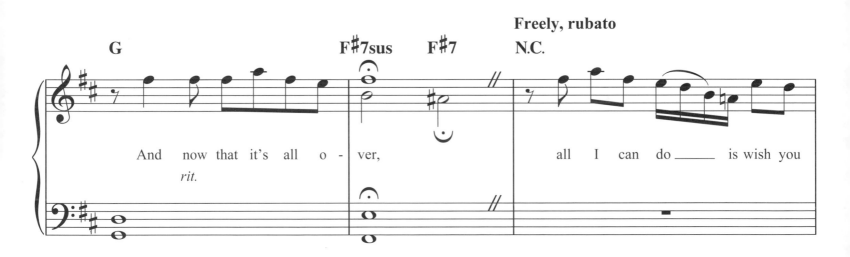